IBC26633

Organizational and Budgetary Slack

ORGANIZATIONAL AND BUDGETARY SLACK —————

AHMED RIAHI-BELKAOUI

Q

QUORUM BOOKS
Westport, Connecticut
London

HF
5549
.5
.M63
R53
1994

Library of Congress Cataloging-in-Publication Data
Riahi-Belkaoui, Ahmed.
    Organizational and budgetary slack / Ahmed Riahi-Belkaoui.
        p.   cm.
    Includes bibliographical references and index.
    ISBN 0–89930–884–8 (alk. paper)
    1. Employee motivation.   2. Organizational behavior.   3. Budget in
business.   I. Title.
    HF5549.5.M63R53   1994
    658.3'14—dc20   93–30990

British Library Cataloguing in Publication Data is available.

Library of Congress Catalog Card Number: 93–30990
ISBN: 0–89930–884–8

First published in 1994

Quorum Books, 88 Post Road West, Westport, CT 06881
An imprint of Greenwood Publishing Group, Inc.

Printed in the United States of America

The paper used in this book complies with the
Permanent Paper Standard issued by the National
Information Standards Organization (Z39.48—1984).

10 9 8 7 6 5 4 3 2 1

To Hedi
Who managed to break his arm while I
was writing this book.

Contents

Exhibits and Figure

FIGURE

Preface

Slack arises from the tendency of organizations and individuals to refrain from using all the resources available to them. It describes a tendency to not operate at peak efficiency. A differentiation is generally made between organizational slack and budgetary slack. Organizational slack refers to the unused resources that are either absorbed as extra expenses or unabsorbed as actual or recoverable liquidity. Budgetary slack arises in the budgeting process and involves the intentional distortion of input information that results from an understatement of budgeted sales and an overstatement of budgeted costs. Organizatonal slack and budgetary slack are organizational phenomena that need to be explicated, identified, controlled, and/or tolerated to allow for a better management of the resources of the firm. The main objective of the book is to explicate both organizational slack and budgetary slack (chapter 1), to explore the properties of organizational slack in the U.S. context (chapter 2), to examine the impact of multidivisional structure and diversification strategy on the creation of organizational slack (chapter 3), to consider the impact of performance plan adoption on the behavior of organizational slack (chapter 4), to determine the impact of self-esteem on budgetary slack (chapter 5), and to evaluate the impact of accountability and self-monitoring on budgetary slack (chapter 6).

The book should be of interest to a variety of readers, including researchers in the field of behavioral accounting and management accounting, management accountants and business executives involved in the management and control of both types of slack, and graduate and undergraduate students in accounting and management.

Many people helped in the development of this book. Jude Grant, Pat Steele, and Eric Valentine of Greenwood Press and Sarah Yu from the University of Illinois at Chicago are true professionals. They have my best gratitude. Finally, thanks to Hedi and Janice M. Belkaoui, whose sense of humor and love made everything possible.

Organizational and Budgetary Slack

1

Organizational and Budgetary Slack

1.1 INTRODUCTION

Richard M. Cyert and James G. March advanced the concept of organizational slack as a hypothetical construct to explain overall organizational phenomena.[1] Arie Y. Lewin and Carl Wolf, on the other hand, have made the following warning: "Slack is a seductive concept; it 'explains' too much and 'predicts' too little."[2] Indeed, slack research needs to be categorized along more precise dimensions that better explain its nature and its impact. Accordingly, this chapter reviews the research on slack by differentiating between *organizational slack* and *budgetary slack*.

1.2 VIEWS OF SLACK

Slack arises from the tendency of organizations and individuals to refrain from using all the resources available to them. It describes a tendency to not operate at peak efficiency. In general, two types of slack have been identified in the literature, namely organizational slack and budgetary slack. Organizational slack basically refers to an unused capacity, in the sense that the demands put on the resources of the organization are less than the supply of these resources. Budgetary slack is found in the budgetary process and refers to the intentional distortion of information that results from an understatement of budgeted sales and an overstatement of budgeted costs.

The concepts of organizational slack and budgetary slack appear in other literature under different labels. Economists refer to an X-inefficiency in instances where resources are either not used to their full capacity or effectiveness or are used in an extremely wasteful manner, as well as in instances where managers fail to make costless improvements. X-inefficiency is to be differentiated from allocative inefficiency, which refers to whether or not prices in a market are of the right kind, that is, whether they allocate input and output to those users who are willing to pay for them.[3] Categories of inefficiency of a nonallocative nature, or X-inefficiency, include inefficiency in (1) labor utilization, (2) capital utilization, (3) time sequence, (4) extent of employee cooperation, (5) information flow, (6) bargaining effectiveness, (7) credit availability utilization, and (8) heuristic procedures.[4]

Agency theory also refers to slack behavior. The problem addressed by the agency theory literature is how to design an incentive contract such that the total gains can be maximized, given (1) information asymmetry between principal and agent, (2) pursuit of self-interest by the agent, and (3) environmental uncertainty affecting the outcome of the agent's decisions.[5] Slack can occur when managers dwell in an "excess consumption of perquisites" or in a "tendency to shrink." Basically, slack is the possible "shrinking" behavior of an agent.[6]

The literature in organizational behavior refers to slack in terms of defensive, tactical responses and deceptive behavior. By viewing organizations as political environments, the deceptive aspects of individual power-acquisition behavior become evident.[7] A variety of unobtrusive tactics in the operation of power,[8] covert intents and means of those exhibiting power-acquisition behaviors,[9] and a "wolf in sheep's clothing" phenomenon, whereby individuals profess a mission or goal strategy while practicing an individual-maximization strategy,[10] characterize these deceptive behaviors, which are designed to present an illusionary or false impression. V. E. Schein has provided the following examples of deceptive behaviors in communication, decision making, and presentation of self.

Communication. With regards to written or oral communications, there may be an illusion that these communications include all the information or that these communications are true, which masks the reality either of them consisting of only partial information or of their actually distorting the information.

Decision making. A manager may present the illusion that he is actually compromising or giving in with regard to a decision, whereas in reality he is purposely planning to lose this particular battle with the long-range objective of winning the war. Or a manager or a subunit may initiate a particular action and then work on plans and activities for implementing a program. This intensive planning and studying, however, may in reality be nothing more than a delaying tactic, during which delay the actual program will die or be forgotten. Underlying this illusion that one is selecting subordinates, members of boards of directors, or successors on the basis of their competency may be the reality that these individuals are selected for loyalty, compliancy, or conformity to the superior's image.

Presentation of self. Many managers exude an apparent confidence, when in reality they are quite uncertain. Still other managers are skilled in organizing participatory group decision-making sessions, which in reality have been set up to produce a controlled outcome.[11]

Schein then hypothesized that the degree to which these behaviors are deceptive seems to be a function of both the nature of the organization and of the kinds of power exhibited (work-related or personal).[12] She relied on Cyert and March's dichotomization of organizations as either low- or high-slack systems.[13] Low-slack systems are characterized by a highly competitive environment that requires rapid and nonroutine decision making on the part of its members and a high level of productive energy and work outcomes to secure an effective performance. High-slack systems are characterized by a reasonably stable environment that requires routine decision making to secure an effective performance. Given these dichotomizations, Schein suggested that:

1. The predominant form of power acquisition behavior is personal in a high-slack organization and work-related in a low-slack organization.

2. The underlying basis of deception is an inherent covert nature of personal power acquisition behaviors in a high-slack organization and an organization['s] illusion as to how work gets done in a low-slack organization.

3. The benefits of deception to members are the provisions of excitement and personal rewards in a high-slack organization and the facilitation of work accomplishment and organizational rewards in a low-slack organization.

4. The benefits of deception to organization are to foster [the] illusion of a fast-paced, competitive environment in a high-slack organization and to maintain an illusion of workability of the formal structure in a low-slack organization.[14]

1.3 ORGANIZATIONAL SLACK

1.3.1 Nature of Organizational Slack

There is no lack of definitions for organizational slack, as can be seen from the definitions provided by Cyert and March,[15] Child,[16] M. D. Cohen, March, and J. P. Olsen,[17] March and Olsen,[18] D. E. Dimmick and V. V. Murray,[19] R. J. Litschert and T. W. Bonham,[20] and March,[21] and as shown in Exhibit 1.1.

What appears from these definitions is that organizational slack is a buffer created by management in its use of available resources to deal with internal as well as external events that may arise and threaten an established coalition. Slack, therefore, is used by management as an agent of change in response to changes in both the internal and external environments.

Cyert and March's model explains slack in terms of cognitive and structural factors.[22] It provides the rationale for the unintended creation of slack. Individuals are assumed to "satisfice," in the sense that they set aspiration levels for performance rather than a maximization goal. These aspirations adjust upward or downward, depending on actual performance, and in a slower fashion than actual changes in performance. It is this lag in adjustment that allows excess re-

Exhibit 1.1
Definitions of Organizational Slack

Cyert & March [1963]

"[The] disparity between the resources available to the organization and the payments required to maintain the coalition" [p. 36].

E.g.: Excess dividends to stockholders

Prices lower than necessary to keep buyers

Wages greater than needed to keep labor

Perquisites to executives

Subunit growth beyond relative rate of contribution

"Supply of uncommitted resources" [p. 54].

"Resources funneled into the satisfaction of individual and sub-group [vs. organizational] objectives" [p. 98].

Child [1972]

"The margin or surplus [performance exceeding "satisficing" level] which permits an organization's dominant coalition to adopt structural arrangements which accord with their own preferences [vs. "goodness of fit" dictates of contingency theory], even at some extra administrative cost" [p. 11].

Cohen, March, & Olsen [1972]

"The difference between the resources of the organization and the combination of demands made on it" [p. 12].

March & Olsen [1976]

"The difference between existing resources and activated demands" [p. 87].

Dimmick & Murray [1978]

"Those resources which an organization has acquired which are not committed to a necessary expenditure. In essence, these are resources which can be used in a discretionary manner" [p. 616].

Operation = Avg. profit over 5 yrs., controlled for size ($ sales)

Litschert & Bonham [1978]

Using Cyert and March's [1963] definition, they gave the following suggested operation: Slack = the variation, from the average among comparable organizations on: ROE, ROTA, Net Sales, and Gross Profit as a percentage of Sales.

March [1979]

"Since organizations do not always optimize, they accumulate spare resources and unexploited opportunities which then become a buffer against bad times. Although the buffer is not necessarily intended, slack produces performance smoothing, reducing performance during good times and improving it during bad times" [quoted in *Stanford GSB*, p. 17].

Source: L. J. Bourgeois, "On the Measurement of Organizational Slack," *Academy of Management Review* 6, no. 1 (1981): 30. Reprinted with permission.

sources from superior performance to accumulate in the form of organizational slack. This slack is then used as a stabilizing force to absorb excess resources in good times without requiring a revision of aspirations and intentions regarding the use of these excess resources. "By absorbing excess resources it retards upward adjustment of aspirations during relatively good times . . . by providing a pool of emergency resources, it permits aspirations to be maintained during relatively bad times."[23]

Oliver E. Williamson has proposed a model of slack based on managerial incentives.[24] This model provides the rationale for managers' motivation and desire for slack resources. Under conditions where managers are able to pursue their own objectives, the model predicts that the excess resources available after target levels of profit have been reached are not allocated according to profit-maximization rules. Organizational slack becomes the means by which a manager achieves his or her personal goals, as characterized by four motives: income, job security, status, and discretionary control over resources. Williamson makes the assumption that the manager is motivated to maximize his or her personal goals subject to satisfying organizational objectives and that the manager achieves this by maximizing slack resources under his or her control. Williamson has suggested that there are four levels of profits: (1) a maximizing profit equal to the profit the firm would achieve when marginal revenue equals marginal cost, (2) actual profit equal to the true profit achieved by the firm, (3) reported profit equal to the accounting profit reported in the annual report, and (4) minimum profit equal to the profit needed to maintain the organizational coalition. If the market is noncompetitive, various forms of slack emerge: (1) *slack absorbed as staff* equal to the difference between maximum profit and actual profit, (2) *slack in the form of cost* equal to the difference between reported and minimum profits, and (3) *discretionary spending for investment* equal to the difference between reported and minimum profits.

Income smoothing can be used to substantiate the efforts of management to neutralize environmental uncertainty and to create organizational slack by means of an accounting manipulation of the level of earnings. J. Y. Kamin and J. Ronen have related organizational slack to income smoothing by reasoning that the decisions that affect the allocation of costs—such as budget negotiations, which often result in slack accumulation—are aimed at smoothing earnings.[25] They hypothesized that management-controlled firms were more likely to be engaged in smoothing as a manifestation of managerial discretion and slack. "Accounting" and "real" smoothing were tested by observing the behavior of discretionary expenses vis-à-vis the behavior of income numbers. Their results showed that (1) a majority of the firms behaved as if they were income smoothers and (2) a particularly strong majority was found among management-controlled firms with high barriers to entry. This line of reasoning was pursued by Ahmed Belkaoui and R. D. Picur.[26] Their study tested the effects of the dual economy on income-smoothing behavior. It was hypothesized that a higher degree of smoothing of income numbers would be exhibited by firms in the periphery sector than by firms in the core sector in reaction to different opportunity structures and experiences. Their results indicated that a majority of the firms may have been resorting to income smoothing. A higher number were found among firms in the periphery sector.

Lewin and Wolf proposed the following statements as a theoretical framework for understanding the concept of slack:

1. Organizational slack depends on the availability of excess resources.

2. Excess resources occur when an organization generates or has the potential to generate resources in excess of what is necessary to maintain the organizational coalition.

3. Slack occurs unintentionally as result of the imperfection of the resource allocation decision-making process.

4. Slack is created intentionally because managers are motivated to maximize slack resources under their control to ensure achievement of personal goals subject to the achievement of organizational goals.

5. The disposition of slack resources is a function of a manager's expense preference function.

6. The distribution of slack resources is an outcome of the bargaining process setting organization and reflects the discretionary power of organization members in allocating resources.

7. Slack can be present in a distributed or concentrated form.

8. The aspiration of organizational participants for slack adjusts upward as resources become available. The downward adjustment of aspirations for slack resources, when resources become scarce, is resisted by organizational participants.

9. Slack can stabilize short-term fluctuations in the firm's performance.

10. Beyond the short term, the reallocation of slack requires a change in organizational goals.

11. Slack is directly related to organizational size, maturity, and stability of the external environment.[27]

1.3.2 Functions of Organizational Slack

Because the definition of slack is often intertwined with a description of the functions that slack serves, L. J. Bourgeois discussed these functions as a means of making palpable the ways of measuring slack.[28] From a review of the administrative theory literature, he identified organizational slack as an independent variable that either "causes" or serves four primary functions: "(1) as an inducement for organizational actors to remain in the system, (2) as a resource for conflict resolution, (3) as a buffering mechanism in the work flow process, or (4) as

Exhibit 1.2
Functions of Slack for Internal Maintenance

	Inducement (to maintain the coalition)	Conflict Resolution	Work flow Buffer
Authors and Concepts	I/C ratio [Barnard, 1937] I/C >1 [March & Simon, 1958] I > 1 = C [Cyert & March, 1963]	Goal incongruence [Pondy, 1967] Local rationality, goal conflict, local optimization [Cyert & March, 1963]	Technical core buffer (inven- tories, adver- tising) [Thompson, 1967] Systems model [Pondy, 1967] Reduced information- processing require- ments [Galbraith, 1973]
Operation	I = Excess dividends Low prices High wages Income and prestige Executive "perks"	Pursuit of pet projects Lowered ROI hurdle Increased/decreased financial authority	Δ in inventory Δ in administrative intensity * * * Reduced performance levels Longer delivery times Hire more labor Buy more equipment
Unit of Analysis	Individual (Σ for organization)	Subunit	Organization
Data Source	Questionnaire	Archival	Archival
Measure	$: static (one point in time)	$ or : relative (compared to previous period)	$: relative Time Labor intensity Static Excess capacity
Problems	Perceptual data Threatening Individual (vs. organi- zational) phenomenon	Sensitive data Subunit slack ≠ organi- zational slack	Slack consumption vs. slack creation

$ = Quantified in terms of monetary value

Δ = Change

Source: L. J. Bourgeois, "On the Measurement of Organizational Slack," *Academy of Management Review* 6, no. 1 (1981): 32. Reprinted with permission.

a facilitator of certain types of strategic or creative behavior within the organization."[29] Exhibit 1.2 summarizes basic information on the first three of these
functions.

The concept of slack as an inducement to maintain the coalition was first introduced by C. I. Barnard in his treatment of the inducement/contribution ratio
(I/C) as a way of attracting organizational participants and sustaining their membership.[30] March and H. A. Simon later described slack resources as the source
of inducements through which the inducement/contribution ratio might exceed
a value of one, which is equivalent to paying an employee more than would be
required to retain his or her services.[31] This concept of slack was then explicitly
introduced by Cyert and March as consisting of payments to members of the
coalition in excess of what is required to maintain the organization.[32]

Slack as a resource for conflict resolution was introduced in L. R. Pondy's goal model.[33] In this model subunit goal conflicts are resolved partly by sequential attention to goals and partly by adopting a decentralized organizational structure. A decentralized structure is made possible by the presence of organizational slack.

A notion of slack as a technical buffer from the variances and discontinuities caused by environmental uncertainty was proposed by J. D. Thompson.[34] It was also acknowledged in Pondy's system model, which described conflict as a result of the lack of buffers between interdependent parts of an organization.[35] Jay Galbraith saw buffering as an information processing problem: "Slack resources are an additional cost to the organization or the customer. . . . The creation of slack resources, through reduced performance levels, reduces the amount of information that must be processed during task execution and prevents the overloading of hierarchical channels."[36]

According to Bourgeois, slack facilitates three types of strategic or creative behavior within the organization: (1) providing resources for innovative be-

Exhibit 1.3
Slack as a Facilitator of Strategic Behavior

	Innovation	Satisficing	Politics
Authors and Concepts	Experimentation with new strategies [Hambrick & Snow, 1977] Funds for innovation [Cyert & March, 1963]	Bounded search [Simon, 1957; March & Simon, 1958]	Bargaining activity [Cyert & March, 1963] Self-aggrandizement; conflict and coalition [Astley, 1978]
Operations	New products New markets New processes R&D and market research	Search time Search team Number of alternatives generated or considered	New resource infusion and subsequent distribution Policy conflicts between managers, coalition formation
Unit of Analysis	Organization	Organization or top management team	Organization or top management team
Data Source	Archival Interview	Interview	Archival Interview Organization

Measure	Products
	Clients, longitu-
	   region dinal
	$: static
		Time
		$ longitudinal
		Process
			$
			                longitu-
			Behavior dinal

$ = Quantified in terms of monetary value

Δ = Change

Source: L. J. Bourgeois, "On the Measurement of Organizational Slack," *Academy of Management Review* 6, no. 1 (1981): 35. Reprinted with permission.

havior, (2) providing opportunities for a satisficing behavior, and (3) affecting political behavior.[37] Exhibit 1.3 summarizes the fundamental characteristics of these types of behavior and their strategic implications for the organization.

First, as a facilitator of innovative behavior, slack tends to create conditions that allow the organization to experiment with new strategies[38] and introduce innovation.[39] Second, as a facilitator of suboptimal behavior, slack defines the threshold of acceptability of a choice, or "bounded search,"[40] by people whose bounded rationality leads them to satisfice.[41] Third, the notion that slack affects political activity was advanced by Cyert and March, who argued that slack reduces both political activity and the need for bargaining and coalition-forming activity.[42] Furthermore, W. G. Astley has argued that slack created by success results in self-aggrandizing behavior by managers who engage in political behavior to capture more than their fair share of the surplus.[43]

W. Richard Scott argued that lowered standards create slack—unused resources—that can be used to create ease in the system.[44] Notice the following comment: "Of course, some slack in the handling of resources is not only inevitable but essential to smooth operations. All operations require a margin of error to allow for mistakes, waste, spoilage, and similar unavoidable accompaniments of work."[45] But the inevitability of slack is not without consequences:

> The question is not whether there is to be slack but how much slack is permitted. Excessive slack resources increase costs for the organization that are likely to be passed on to the consumer. Since creating slack resources is a relatively easy and painless solution available to organizations, whether or not it is employed is likely to be determined by the amount of competition confronting the organization in its task environment.[46]

1.3.3 Measurement of Organizational Slack

One problem in investing empirically the presence of organizational slack relates to the difficulty of securing an adequate measurement of the phenomenon. As Exhibits 1.2 and 1.3 show, various methods have been suggested. In addition to these methods, eight variables that appear in public data, whether they are created by managerial actions or made available by environment, may explain a change in slack.[47] The model, suggested by Bourgeois, is as follows:

$$\text{Slack} = f(\text{RE, DP, G\&A, WC/S, D/E, CR, I/P, P/E})$$

where

RE   = Retained earnings
DP   = Dividend payout
G&A = General and administrative expense
WC/S = Working capital as a percentage of sales

D/E   = Debt as a percentage of equity
CR   = Credit rating
I/P   = Short-term loan interest compared to prime rate
P/E   = Price/earnings ratio.

Here RE, G&A, WC/S, and CR are assumed to have a positive effect on changes in slack, whereas DP, D/E, P/E, and I/P are assumed to have a negative effect on changes in slack.

Some of these measures have also been suggested by other researchers. For example, Martin M. Rosner used profit and excess capacity as slack measures,[48] and Lewin and Wolf used selling, general, and administrative expenses as surrogates for slack.[49] Bourgeois and Jitendra V. Singh refined these measures by suggesting that slack could be differentiated on an "ease-or-recovery" dimension.[50] Basically, they considered excess liquidity to be *available slack*, not yet earmarked for particular uses. Overhead costs were termed *recoverable slack*, in the sense that they are absorbed by various organizational functions but can be recovered when needed elsewhere. In addition, the ability of a firm to generate resources from the environment, such as the ability to raise additional debt or equity capital, was considered *potential slack*. All of these measures were divided by sales to control for company size.

Building on Bourgeois and Singh's suggestions, Theresa K. Lant opted for the four following measures:

1. Administrative Slack = (General and Administrative Expenses)/Cost of Goods Sold

2. Available Liquidity = (Cash + Marketable Securities – Current Liabilities)/Sales

3. Recoverable Liquidity = (Accounts Receivable + Inventory)/Sales

4. Retained Earnings = (Net Profit – Dividends)/Sales.[51]

Lant used these measures to show empirically that (1) available liquidity and general and administrative expenses have significantly higher variance than profit across firms and across time and (2) the mean change in slack is significantly greater than the mean change in profit. She concluded as follows:

These results are logically consistent with the theory that slack absorbs variance in actual profit. They also suggest that the measures used are reasonable measures for slack. Thus, it supports prior work which has used these measures, and implies that further large sample models using slack as a variable is feasible since financial information is readily available for a large number of firms. Before these results can be generalized, however, the tests conducted here should be replicated using different samples of firms from a variety of industries.[52]

1.4 BUDGETARY SLACK

1.4.1 Nature of Budgetary Slack

The literature on organizational slack shows that managers have the motives necessary to desire to operate in a slack environment. The literature on budgetary slack considers the budget as the embodiment of that environment and, therefore, assumes that managers will use the budgeting process to bargain for slack budgets. As stated by Michael Schiff and Lewin, "managers will create slack in budgets through a process of *understating revenues and overstating costs*."[53] The general, definition of budgetary slack, then, is the understatement of revenues and the overstatement of costs in the budgeting process. A detailed description of the creation of budgetary slack by managers was reported by Schiff and Lewin in their study of the budget process of three divisions of multidivision companies.[54] They found evidence of budgetary slack through underestimation of gross revenue, inclusion of discretionary increases in personnel requirements, establishment of marketing and sales budgets with internal limits on funds to be spent, use of manufacturing costs based on standard costs that do not reflect process improvements operationally available at the plant, and inclusion of discretionary "special projects."

Evidence of budgetary slack has also been reported by others. A. E. Lowe and R. W. Shaw found a downward bias, introduced through sales forecasts by line managers, which assumed good performance where rewards were related to forecasts.[55] M. Dalton reported various examples of department managers allocating resources to what they considered justifiable purposes even though such purposes were not authorized in their budgets.[56] G. Shillinglaw noted the extreme vulnerability of budgets used to measure divisional performance given the great control exercised by divisional management in budget preparation and the reporting of results.[57]

Slack creation is a generalized organizational phenomenon. Many different organizational factors have been used to explain slack creation, in particular, organizational structure, goal congruence, control system, and managerial behavior. Slack creation is assumed to occur in cases where a Tayloristic organizational structure exists,[58] although it is also assumed to occur in a participative organizational structure.[59] It may be due to conflicts that arise between the individual and organizational goals, leading managers intentionally to create slack. It may also be due to the attitudes of management toward the budget and to workers' views of the budgets as a device used by management to manipulate them.[60] Finally, the creation of slack may occur whether or not the organization is based on a centralized or decentralized structure.[61] With regard to this last issue, Schiff and Lewin have reported that the divisional controller appears to have undertaken the tasks of creating and managing divisional slack and is most influential in the internal allocation of slack.

1.4.2 Budgeting and the Propensity to Create Budgetary Slack

The budgeting system has been assumed to affect a manager's propensity to create budgetary slack, in the sense that this propensity can be increased or decreased by the way in which the budgeting system is designed or complemented. Mohamed Onsi was the first to investigate empirically the connections between the type of budgeting system and the propensity to create budgetary slack.[62] From a review of the literature, he stated the following four assumptions:

1. Managers influence the budget process through bargaining for slack by understating revenues and overstating costs. . . .

2. Managers build up slack in "good years" and reconvert slack into profit in "bad years." . . .

3. Top management is at a "disadvantage" in determining the magnitude of slack. . . .

4. The divisional controller in decentralized organizations participates in the task of creating and managing divisional slack.[63]

Personal interviews of thirty-two managers of five large, national and international companies and statistical analysis of a questionnaire were used to identify the important behavioral variables that influence slack buildup and utilization. The questionnaire's variables were grouped into the following eight dimensions:

1. *Slack attitude* described by the variables indicating a manager's attitude to slack.

2. *Slack manipulation* described by the variables indicating how a manager builds up and uses slack.

3. *Slack institutionalization* described by the variables that make a manager less inclined to reduce his slack.

4. *Slack detection* described by the variables indicating the superior's ability to detect slack based on the amount of information he receives.

5. *Attitude toward the top management control system* described by the variables indicating an authoritarian philosophy toward budgeting being attributed to top management by divisional managers.

6. *Attitudes toward the divisional control system* described by variables on attitudes toward subordinates, sources of pressure, budget autonomy, budget participation, and supervisory uses of budgets.

7. *Attitudes toward the budget described* by variables on attitude toward the level of standards, attitude towards the relevancy of budget attain-

ment to valuation of performance, and the manager's attitude (positive or negative) toward the budgetary system in general, as a managerial tool.

8. *Budget relevancy* described by variables indicating a manager's attitudes toward the relevancy of standards for his department's operation.[64]

The questionnaire is shown in Exhibit 1.4.

Factor analysis reduced these dimensions to seven factors and showed a relationship between budgetary slack and what Onsi called "an authoritarian top management budgetary control system." Thus, he stated: "Budgetary slack is created as a result of pressure and the use of budgeted profit attainment as a basic criterion in evaluating performance. Positive participation could encourage less need for building-up slack. However, the middle managers' perception of pressure was an overriding concern. The positive correlation between managers' attitudes and attainable level of standards is a reflection of this pressure."[65]

Cortland and Cammann explored the moderating effects of subordinates' participation in decision making and the difficulty of subordinates' jobs based on their responses to different uses of control systems by their superiors.[66] His results showed that the use of control systems for contingent reward allocation produced defensive responses by subordinates under all conditions, which included the creation of budgetary slack. Basically, when superiors used budgeting information as a basis for allocating organizational rewards, their subordinates' responses were defensive. Allowing participation in the budget processes reduced this defensiveness.

Finally, Kenneth A. Merchant conducted a field study designed to investigate how managers' propensities to create budgetary slack are affected by the budgeting system and the technical context.[67] He hypothesized that the propensity to create budgetary slack is positively related to the importance placed on meeting budget targets and negatively related to the extent of participation allowed in budgeting processes, the degree of predictability in the production process, and the superiors' abilities to create slack. Unlike earlier studies that had drawn across functional areas, 170 manufacturing managers responded to a questionnaire measuring the propensity to create slack, the importance of meeting the budget, budget participation, the nature of technology in terms of work-flow integration and product standardization, and the ability of superiors to detect slack. The results suggested that managers' propensities to create slack (1) do vary with the setting and with how the budgeting system is implemented; (2) are lower where managers actively participate in budgeting, particularly when technologies are relatively predictable; and (3) are higher when a tight budget requires frequent tactical responses to avoid overruns.

The three studies by Onsi, Cammann, and Merchant, provide evidence that participation may lead to positive communication between managers so that

Exhibit 1.4

Questionnaire Items Arranged within the Dimensions of the a priori Structure

1. Slack attitude

26. To protect himself, a manager submits a budget that can safely be attained.
27. The plant manager sets two levels of standards: one between himself and production (sales) manager, and another standard between himself and top management, to be safe.
30. In good business times, the plant manager accepts a reasonable level of slack in a departmental budget.
41. Slack in the budget is good to do things that cannot be officially approved.

2. Slack manipulation

24. With some skill, a manager can make his performance unit just as he wants.
43. The plant controller is "considerate" to the departmental manager who needs to attain the budget.

3. Slack institutionalization

31. In bad business times, the most profitable department in the past is less inclined to reduce its "slack" than other departments that show less profit.
33. The manager who has been on the job for a long time is less inclined than a new manager to reduce his "slack" by cutting expenditures.
34. The manager who has a strong personality will be less inclined to reduce "slack" in his budget.

4. Slack detection

28. The plant manager has enough information to know if there is slack in a departmental budget.
40. Top management receives detailed information on the plant activities by department and product.
42. Top management has a way to know if there is slack in a departmental budget.

5. Attitude toward top management control systems

35. Top management judges the plant performance *only* on the basis of attaining budget profits.
37. Top management hates nothing more than a plant manager failing to meet his budget.
38. Top management believes in the merits of exerting pressure on middle management.
39. If a plant manager fails in attaining his budget, top management takes the position that he should be replaced.

6. Attitude toward subordinates

10. My subordinates learn that obedience and respect for authority are the most important virtues.
13. A clear order to subordinates is better than consultation.
16. Subordinates ought to accept their boss's decisions without reservation.
17. If people would talk less and work more everybody would be better off.

7. Pressure

23. I pressure my subordinates to get things done for corporate benefits first.
32. The budget in my department is set at a "tight" level to put on pressure for increasing productivity and cost control.

8. Budget autonomy

4. The budget is primarily developed to meet my department's interest first.
20. My boss accepts my budgets without reservation.
22. I have complete autonomy in making decisions related to my departmental budget.

9. Budget participation (and communication)

25. I receive "goals" from top management that I use as a basis for developing the departmental budget.
2. I attend meetings of line management where budget variances are discussed.
21. My boss listens to my ideas for improving the budget and increasing productivity.
9. In this plant my private interests are taken account of as much as possible.

10. Supervisory uses of budget

1. My boss works with budgetary figures in making decisions.

Exhibit 1.4   (Continued)

12. My boss emphasizes cost reduction.
14. My boss evaluates my department's attaining the budget with me.
11. Attitude toward standard level
 3. I prefer a standard that can be attained.
44. A manager would rather overattain the budget than underattain it.
12. Attitude toward relevancy of budget attainment to evaluation
18. Monetary incentives are primarily tied to attaining the budget.
19. If I do not attain the budget, my boss gets upset.
15. In evaluating a manager, his ability to get things done through his subordinates receives high importance.
13. Budget attitude (general)
 7. Budgeting is first of all an accounting tool.
11. I think trying to attain the budget is a game.
14. Budget relevancy
 5. The standards that are set induce higher productivity in my department.
 6. If given a choice, I would prefer to work without standards.
 8. If no standards were set, but instructions would be to work as efficiently as possible, this would make my department's performance higher than it is now.

Source: Mohamed Onsi, "Behavioral Variables Affecting Budgetary Slack," *The Accounting Review* (July 1973): 547–548. Reprinted with permission.

subordinates feel less pressure to create slack. This result is, in fact, contingent on the amount of information asymmetry existing between the principals (superiors) and the agents (the subordinates). Although participation in budgeting leads subordinates to communicate or reveal some of their private information, agents may still misrepresent or withhold some of their private information, leading to budgetary slack. Accordingly, Alan S. Dunk proposed a link between participation and budgetary slack through two variables: superiors' budget emphasis in their evaluation of subordinate performance and the degree of information asymmetry between superiors and subordinates[68]: "When participation, budget emphasis, and information asymmetry are high (low), slack will be high (low)."[69] Exhibits 1.5 and 1.6 show the instruments used to measure budgetary slack and information asymmetry. The results, however, showed that low (high) slack is related to high (low) participation, budget emphasis and information asymmetry. The results are stated as follows:

> The results of this study show that the relation between participation and slack is contingent upon budget emphasis and information asymmetry, but in a direction contrary to expectations. The results provide evidence for the utility of participative budgeting, and little support for the view that high participation may result in increased slack when the other two predictors are high. Although participation may induce subordinates to incorporate slack in budgets, the results suggest that participation alone may not be sufficient. The findings suggest that slack reduction results from participation, except when budget emphasis is low.[70]

Exhibit 1.5
Budgetary Slack Measure

The following statements relate to the budgetary environment in which you work.
Please indicate the extent of your agreement with each statement by circling a
number from 1 to 7, based on the following scale:

 1. Strongly disagree   5. Mildly agree

 2. Moderately disagree   6. Moderately agree

 3. Mildly disagree   7. Strongly agree

 4. Neutral

1. Standards set in the budget induce high   1 2 3 4 5 6 7
   productivity in my area of responsibility.*

2. Budgets set for my area of responsibility   1 2 3 4 5 6 7
   are safely attainable.

3. I have to carefully monitor costs in my   1 2 3 4 5 6 7
   area of responsibility because of bud-
   getary constraints.*

4. Budgets for my area of responsibility are   1 2 3 4 5 6 7
   not particularly demanding.

5. Budgetary targets have not caused me to   1 2 3 4 5 6 7
   be particularly concerned with improving
   efficiency in my area of responsibility.

6. Targets incorporated in the budget are   1 2 3 4 5 6 7
   difficult to reach.*

* Responses to these items were reverse-scored.

Source: Alan S. Dunk, "The Effect of Budget Emphasis and Information Asymmetry on the Relation Between Budgetary Participation and Slack," *The Accounting Review* (April 1993): 408.
Reprinted with permission.

1.4.3 Budgetary Slack, Information Distortion, and
Truth-Inducing Incentives Schemes

Budgetary slack involves a deliberate distortion of input information. Distortion of input information in a budget setting arises, in particular, from the need
of managers to accommodate their expectations about the kinds of payoffs associated with different possible outcomes. Several experiments have provided evidence of such distortion of input information. Cyert, March, and W. H.
Starbuck showed in a laboratory experiment that subjects adjusted the information they transmitted in a complex decision-making system to control their pay-

Exhibit 1.6
Information Asymmetry Measure

Please respond to each of the following questions by circling a number from 1 to 7, based on their individual scales:

1. In comparison with your superior, who is in possession of better information regarding the activities undertaken in your area of responsibility?

1	2	3	4	5	6	7
My superior has much better information			We have about the same quality of information			I have much better information

2. In comparison with your superior, who is more familiar with the input-output relationships inherent in the internal operations of your area of responsibility?

1	2	3	4	5	6	7
My superior is much more familiar			We are about equally familiar			I am much more familiar

3. In comparison with your superior, who is more certain of the performance potential of your area of responsibility?

1	2	3	4	5	6	7
My superior is much more certain			We are about equally certain			I am much more certain

4. In comparison with your superior, who is more familiar technically with the work of your area of responsibility?

1	2	3	4	5	6	7
My superior is much more familiar			We are about equally familiar			I am much more familiar

(continued)

Exhibit 1.6   (Continued)

5. In comparison with your superior, who is better able to assess the potential impact on your activities of factors external to your area of responsibility?

```
      1           2           3           4           5           6           7

 My superior is                        We are about                    I am much

 much better able                      equally able                    better able
```

6. In comparison with your superior, who has a better understanding of what can be achieved in your area of responsibility?

```
      1           2           3           4           5           6           7

 My superior has                       We have about                   I have a

 a much better                         the same                        much better

 understanding                         understanding                   understanding
```

Source: Alan S. Dunk, "The Effect of Budget Emphasis and Information Asymmetry on the Relation Between Budgetary Participation and Slack," *The Accounting Review* (April 1993): 408–409. Reprinted with permission.

offs.[71] Similarly, Lowe and Shaw have shown that in cases where rewards were linked to forecasts, sales managers tended to distort the input information and to induce biases in their sales forecast.[72] Dalton also provided some rich situational descriptions of information distortion in which lower level managers distorted the budget information and allocated resources to what were perceived to be justifiable objectives.[73] Finally, given the existence of a payoff structure that can induce a forecaster to bias intentionally his or her forecast, R. M. Barefield provided a model of forecast behavior that showed a "rough" formulation of a possible link between a forecaster's biasing and the quality of the forecaster as a source of data for an accounting system.[74]

Taken together, these studies suggest that budgetary slack, through systematic distortion of input information, can be used to accommodate the subjects' expectations about the payoffs associated with various possible outcomes. They fail, however, to provide a convincing rationalization of the link between distortion of input information and the subjects' accommodation of their expectations. Agency theory and issues related to risk aversion may provide such a link. Hence, given the existence of divergent incentives and information asymmetry between the controller (or employer) and the controllee (or employee) and the high cost of observing employee skill or effort, a budget-based employment contract (that is, where employee compensation is contingent on meeting the performance standard) can be Pareto-superior to fixed pay or linear sharing rules (where the employer and employee split the output).[75] However, these budget-

based schemes impose a risk on the employee, as job performance can be affected by a host of uncontrollable factors. Consequently, risk-averse individuals
may resort to slack budgeting through systematic distortion of input information. In practice, moreover, any enhanced (increased) risk aversion would lead
the employee to resort to budgetary slack. One might hypothesize that, without
proper incentives for truthful communication, the slack budgeting behavior
could be reduced. One suggested avenue is the use of truth-inducing, budget-
based schemes.[76] These schemes, assuming risk neutrality, motivate a worker to
reveal truthfully private information about future performance and to maximize
performance regardless of the budget.

Accordingly, Mark S. Young conducted an experiment to test the effects of
risk aversion and asymmetric information on slack budgeting.[77] Five hypotheses
related to budgetary slack were developed and tested using a laboratory experiment. The hypotheses were as follows:

Hypothesis 1: A subordinate who participates in the budgeting process
will build slack into the budget. . . .

Hypothesis 2: A risk-averse subordinate will build in more budget slack
than a non-risk-averse subordinate. . . .

Hypothesis 3: Social pressure not to misrepresent productive capability
will be greater for a subordinate whose information is known by management than for a subordinate having private information. . . .

Hypothesis 4: As social pressure increases for the subordinate, there is
a lower degree of budgetary slack. . . .

Hypothesis 5: A subordinate who has private information builds more
slack into the budget than a subordinate whose information is known by
management.[78]

The results of the experiment confirmed the hypotheses that a subordinate who
participates builds in budgetary slack and that slack is, in part, attributable to a
subordinate's risk preferences. Given state uncertainty and a worker-manager
information asymmetry about performance capability, the subjects in the experiment created slack even in the presence of a truth-inducing scheme. In addition, risk-averse workers created more slack than non-risk-averse workers did.
Similarly, C. Chow, J. Cooper, and W. Waller provided evidence that, given a
worker-manager information asymmetry about performance capability, slack is
lower under a truth-inducing scheme than under a budget-based scheme with
an incentive to create slack.[79]

Both Young's and Chow, Cooper, and Waller's studies were found to have limitations.[80] With regard to Young's study, William S. Waller found three limitations: "First, unlike the schemes examined in the analytical research, the one
used in his study penalized outperforming the budget, which limits its general
usefulness. Second, there was no manipulation of incentives, so variation in slack
due to incentives was not examined. Third, risk preferences were measured

using the conventional lottery technique of which the validity and reliability are suspect."[81] With regard to Chow, Cooper, and Waller's study, Waller found the limitations to be the assumption of state certainty and the failure to take risk preference into account. Accordingly, Waller conducted an experiment under which subjects participatively set budgets under either a scheme with an incentive for creating slack or a truth-incentive scheme like those examined in the analytical research. In addition, risk neutrality was induced for one half of the subjects and constant, absolute risk aversion for the rest, using a technique discussed by J. Berg, L. Daley, J. Dickhaut, and J. O'Brien that allows the experimenter to induce (derived) utility functions with any shape.[82] The results of the experiment show that when a conventional truth-inducing scheme is introduced, slack decreases for risk-neutral subjects but not for risk-averse subjects. Added to the evidence provided by the other studies, this study indicates that risk preference is an important determinant of slack, especially in the presence of a truth-inducing scheme.

Basically, there is preliminary evidence that risk-averse workers create more budgetary slack than risk-neutral ones. In addition, "truth-inducing incentive schemes" reduce budgetary slack for risk-neutral subjects but not for risk-averse subjects. It seems that resource allocations within organizations are mediated by perceptions of risk, where risk is a stable personal trait. Accordingly, D. C. Kim tested whether risk preferences are domain-specific; that is, latent risk preferences translate into differing manifest risk preferences according to the context.[83] He relied on an experiment simulating the public accountants' budgeting of billable bonus to test the hypothesis that subject preference for tight or safe budget behavior depends on the performance of coworkers and domain-specific risk preferences. The results supported the view that subordinates' risk preferences are influenced by a situation-dependent variable. As stated by Kim: "The reversal of risk preferences around a neutral reference point is statistically significant for both dispositionally risk-averse and dispositionally risk-seeking subjects. The dispositional variable also contributes to the explanation of variations in subjects' manifest risk preferences. Thus the propensity to induce budgetary slack seems to be a joint function of situations and dispositions."[84]

1.4.4 Budgetary Slack and Self-Esteem

The enhancement of risk aversion and the resulting distortion of input information can be more pronounced when self-esteem is threatened. It was found that persons who have low opinions of themselves are more likely to cheat than persons with higher self-esteem.[85] A situation of dissonance was created in an experimental group by giving out positive feedback about a personality test to some participants and negative feedback to others. All the participants were then asked to take part in a competitive game of cards. The participants who received a blow to their self-esteem cheated more often than those who had received positive feedback about themselves. Could it also be concluded that budgetary slack through information distortion may be a form of dishonest behavior, arising from the enhancement of risk aversion caused by a negative feedback on self-esteem? A person's expectations can be an important determinant of his or her behavior. A negative impact on self-esteem can lead an individual to develop an expectation of poor performance. At the same time, the individual who is given negative feedback about his or her self-esteem would be more risk averse than others and would be ready to resort to any behavior to cover the situation. Consequently, the person may attempt to distort the input information in order to have an attainable budget. Belkaoui accordingly tested the hypothesis that individuals given negative feedback about their self-esteem would introduce more bias into estimates than individuals given positive or neutral feedback about their self-esteem.[86] One week after taking a self-esteem test, subjects were provided with false feedback (either positive or negative) and neutral feedback about their self-esteem score. They were then asked to make two budgeting decisions, first one cost estimate and then one sales estimate for a fictional budgeting decision. The results showed that, in general, the individuals who were provided with information that temporarily caused them to lower their self-esteem were more apt to distort input information than those who were made to raise their self-esteem. It was concluded that, whereas slack budgeting may be consistent with generally low self-esteem feedback, it is inconsistent with generally high or neutral self-esteem feedback.

1.4.5 Toward a Theoretical Framework for Budgeting

A theoretical framework aimed at structuring knowledge about biasing behavior was proposed by Kari Lukka.[87] It contains an explanatory model for budgetary biasing and a model for budgetary biasing at the organizational level.

The explanatory model of budgetary biasing at the individual level is presented in Exhibit 1.7. It draws from the management accounting and organizational behavior literature and related behavioral research to suggest a set of intentions and determinants of budgetary biasing. Budgetary biasing is at the center of many interrelated and sometimes contradictory factors with the actor's intentions as the synthetic core of his or her behavior.

The model for budgetary biasing at the organizational level is presented in Exhibit 1.8. It shows that the "bias contained in the final budget is not the result of one actor's intentional behavior, but rather the result of the dialectics of the negotiations."[88] Whereas budgetary biases 1 and 2 are the original biases created in the budget by the controlling unit and the controlled unit, biases 3 and 4 are the final biases to end up in the budget after the budgetary negotiations, which are characterized by potential conflicts and power factors. The results of semi-structured interviews at different levels of management of a large decentralized company verified the theoretical framework. The usefulness of this theoretical framework rests on further refinements and empirical testing.

Exhibit 1.7
Intentions and Determinants of Budgetary Biasing

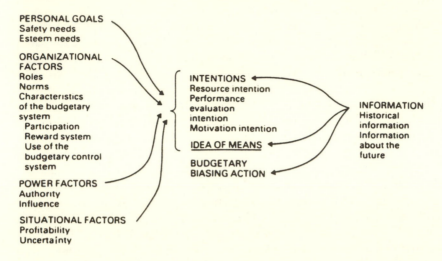

Source: Kari Lukka, "Budgetary Biasing in Organizations: Theoretical Framework and Empirical Evidence," *Accounting, Organizations and Society* (February 1988): 291. Reprinted with permission.

Exhibit 1.8
Budgetary Process from the Biasing Viewpoint

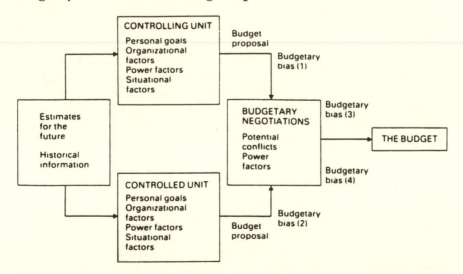

Source: Kari Lukka, "Budgetary Biasing in Organizations: Theoretical Framework and Empirical Evidence," *Accounting, Organizations and Society* (February 1988): 292. Reprinted with permission.

1.4.6 Positive versus Negative Slack

Although the previous sections have focused on budgetary, or positive, slack, budgetary bias is, in fact, composed of both budgetary slack and an upward bias, or a negative slack. Whereas budgetary slack refers to bias in which the budget is designed intentionally so as to make it easier to achieve the forecast, upward bias refers to overstatement of expected performance in the budget. David T. Otley has described the difference as follows: "Managers are therefore likely to be conservative in making forecasts when future benefits are sought (positive slack) but optimistic when their need for obtaining current approval dominates (negative slack)."[89]

Evidence for negative slack was first provided by W. W. Read, who showed that managers distort information to prove to their superiors that all is well.[90] He cited several empirical studies of budgetary control that indicated that managers put a lot of effort and ingenuity into assuring that messages conveyed by budgetary information serve their own interests.[91] Following earlier research by Barefield, Otley argued that forecasts may be the mode, rather than the means, of people's intuitive probability distributions.[92] Given that the distribution of cost and revenue is negatively skewed, there will be a tendency for budget forecasts to become unintentionally biased in the form of negative slack. Data collected from two organizations verified the presence of negative slack.

1.4.7 Reducing Budgetary Slack: A Bonus-Based Technique

In general, firms use budgeting and bonus techniques to overcome slack budgeting. One such approach consists of paying higher rewards when budgets are set high and achieved, and lower rewards when budgets are either set high but not met or set low and achieved. G. S. Mann presented a bonus system that gave incentives for managers to set budget estimates as close to achievable levels as possible.[93] The following two formulas were proposed:

Formula 1 applies for bonus if actual performance is equal to or greater than budget.

$$(\text{multiplier no. 2} \times \text{budget goal}) + [\text{multiplier no. 1} \times (\text{actual level achieved} - \text{budget goal})]$$

Formula 2 applies for bonus if actual performance is less than budget.

$$(\text{multiplier no. 2} \times \text{budget goal}) + [\text{multiplier no. 3} \times (\text{actual level achieved} - \text{budget goal})]$$

The three multipliers set by management served as factors in calculating different components of bonuses. They were defined as follows:

Exhibit 1.9
Reducing Slack through a Bonus System

(1)	(2)	(3)	(4) Bonus I	(5) Bonus II
Budget Sales	Actual Sales	State of Nature	Multiple No. 1 = $.05 Multiple No. 2 = $.10 Multiple No. 3 = $.15	Multiple no. 1 = .01 Multiple no. 2 = .10 Multiple no. 3 = .30
200,000	180,000	Over estimation	$17,000	$14,000
200,000	200,000	Actual = Budget	20,000	20,000
200,000	220,000	Under estimation	21,000	22,000

Multiplier no. 1 (which must be less than multiplier no. 2, and which in turn must be less than multiplier no. 3) is used when actual performance is greater than budget. It provides a smaller bonus per unit for the part of actual performance that exceeds the budgeted amount. . . .

Multiplier no. 2 is the rate per unit used to determine the basic bonus component. It is based on the budgeted level of activity which equals multiplier no. 2 times the budgeted level.

Multiplier no. 3 is the rate used to reduce the bonus when the achieved level is less than the budget (multiplier no. 3 times work of units by which actual performance fell short of budget).[94]

Exhibit 1.9 shows an illustration of the application of the method and the effect of variations in multipliers or bonuses. As the exhibit shows, the manager will be rewarded for accurate estimation of the level of rates. In addition, the multipliers can be set with greater flexibility for controlling the manager's estimates.

1.4.8 Conclusion

Organizational slack and budgetary slack are two hypothetical constructs to explain organizational phenomena that are prevalent in all forms of organizations. Evidence linking both constructs to organizational, individual, and contextual factors is growing and in the future may contribute to an emerging theoretical framework for an understanding of slack. Further investigation into the potential determinants of organizational and budgetary slack remains to be done. This effort is an important one because the behavior of slack is highly relevant to the achievement of internal economic efficiency in organizations. Witness the following comment: "The effective organization has more rewards at its disposal, or more organizational slack to pay with, and thus can allow all members to exercise more discretion, obtain more rewards, and feel that their influence is higher."[95]

NOTES

1. Richard M. Cyert and James G. March, eds., *A Behavioral Theory of the Firm* (Englewood Cliffs, N.J.: Prentice-Hall, 1963).

2. Arie Y. Lewin and Carl Wolf, "The Theory of Organizational Slack: A Critical Review," *Proceedings: Twentieth International Meeting of TIMS* (1976): 648–654.

3. Harvey Leibenstein, "Allocative Efficiency vs. 'X-Efficiency,' " *American Economic Review* (June 1966): 392–415.

4. Harvey Leibenstein, "X-Efficiency: From Concept to Theory," *Challenge* (September-October 1979): 13–22.

5. Nandan Choudhury, "Incentives for the Divisional Manager," *Accounting and Business Research* (Winter 1985): 11–21.

6. S. Baiman, "Agency Research in Managerial Accounting: A Survey," *Journal of Accounting Literature* (Spring 1982): 154–213.

7. D. Packard, *The Pyramid Climber* (New York: McGraw-Hill, 1962); E. A. Buttler, "Corporate Politics—Monster or Friend?" *Generation 3* (1971): 54–58, 74; A. N. Schoomaker, *Executive Career Strategies* (New York: American Management Association, 1971).

8. J. Pfeffer, "Power and Resource Allocation in Organizations," in B. M. Shaw and G. R. Salancik, eds., *New Directions in Organizational Behavior* (Chicago: St. Clair Press, 1977).

9. V. E. Schein, "Individual Power and Political Behaviors in Organizations: An Inadequately Explored Reality," *Academy of Management Review* (January 1977): 64–72.

10. B. Bozeman and W. Malpive, "Goals and Bureaucratic Decision-Making: An Experiment," *Human Relations* (June 1977): 417–429.

11. V. E. Schein, "Examining an Illusion: The Role of Deceptive Behaviors in Organizations," *Human Relations* (October 1979): 288–289.

12. Ibid., p. 290.

13. Cyert and March, *A Behavioral Theory of the Firm.*

14. Schein, "Examining an Illusion," p. 293.

15. Cyert and March, *A Behavioral Theory of the Firm.*

16. John Child, "Organizational Structure, Environment, and Performance: The Role of Strategic Choice," *Sociology* 6, no. 1 (1972): 2–22.

17. M. D. Cohen, J. G. March, and J. P. Olsen, "A Garbage Can Model of Organizational Choice," *Administrative Science Quarterly* 17, no. 1 (1972): 1–25.

18. J. G. March and J. P. Olsen, *Ambiguity and Choice* (Bergen: Universitetsforlagt, 1976).

19. D. E. Dimmick and V. V. Murray, "Correlates of Substantive Policy Decisions in Organizations: The Case of Human Resource Management," *Academy of Management Journal* 21, no. 4 (1978): 611–623.

20. R. J. Litschert and T. W. Bonham, "A Conceptual Model of Strategy Formation," *Academy of Management Review* 3, no. 2 (1978): 211–219.

21. James G. March, interview by Stanford Business School Alumni Association, *Stanford GSB* 47, no. 3 (1978–79): 16–19.

22. Cyert and March, *A Behavioral Theory of the Firm.*

23. Ibid., p. 38.

24. Oliver E. Williamson, "A Model of Rational Managerial Behavior," in Richard M. Cyert and James G. March, eds., *A Behavioral Theory of the Firm* (Englewood Cliffs, N.J.: Prentice-Hall, 1963); idem, *The Economics of Discretionary Behavior: Managerial Objectives in a Theory of the Firm* (Englewood Cliffs, N.J.: Prentice-Hall, 1964).

25. J. Y. Kamin and J. Ronen, "The Smoothing of Income Numbers: Some Empirical Evidence on Systematic Differences among Management-Controlled and Owner-Controlled Firms," *Accounting, Organizations and Society* (October 1978): 141–157.

26. Ahmed Belkaoui and R. D. Picur, "The Smoothing of Income Numbers: Some Empirical Evidence on Systematic Differences between Core and Periphery Industrial Sector," *Journal of Business Finance and Accounting* (Winter 1984): 527–545.

27. Lewin and Wolf, "The Theory of Organizational Slack," p. 653.

28. L. J. Bourgeois, "On the Measurement of Organizational Slack," *Academy of Management Review* 6, no. 1 (1982): 29–39.

29. Ibid., p. 31.

30. C. I. Barnard, *Functions of the Executive* (Cambridge, Mass.: Harvard University Press, 1938).

31. James G. March and H. A. Simon, *Organizations* (New York: John Wiley and Sons, 1958).

32. Cyert and March, *A Behavioral Theory of the Firm*, p. 36.

33. L. R. Pondy, "Organizational Conflict: Concepts and Models," *Administrative Science Quarterly* 12, no. 2 (1967): 296–320.

34. J. D. Thompson, *Organizations in Action* (New York: McGraw-Hill, 1967).

35. Pondy, "Organizational Conflict."

36. Jay Galbraith, *Designing Complex Organizations* (Reading, Mass.: Addison-Wesley, 1973), p. 15.

37. Bourgeois, "On the Measurement of Organizational Slack," p. 34.

38. D. C. Hambrick and C. C. Snow, "A Contextual Model of Strategic Decision Making in Organizations," in R. L. Taylor, J. J. O'Connell, R. A. Zawaki, and D. D. Warrick, eds., *Academy of Management Proceedings* (1977): 109–112.

39. Cyert and March, *A Behavioral Theory of the Firm*.

40. March and Simon, *Organizations*.

41. H. A. Simon, *Administrative Behavior* (New York: Free Press, 1957).

42. Cyert and March, *A Behavioral Theory of the Firm*.

43. W. G. Astley, "Sources of Power in Organizational Life," Ph.D. Diss., University of Washington, 1978.

44. W. Richard Scott, *Organizations: Rational, Natural and Open Systems* (Englewood Cliffs, N. J.: Prentice-Hall, 1981), p. 216.

45. Ibid.

46. Ibid.

47. Bourgeois, "On the Measurement of Organizational Slack," p. 38.

48. Martin M. Rosner, "Economic Determinant of Organizational Innovation," *Administrative Science Quarterly* 12 (1968): 614–625.

49. Arie Y. Lewin and Carl Wolf, "Organizational Slack: A Test of the General Theory," *Journal of Management Studies* (forthcoming).

50. L. J. Bourgeois and Jitendra V. Singh, "Organizational Slack and Political Behavior within Top Management Teams," Working paper, Graduate School of Business, Stanford University, 1983.

51. Theresa K. Lant, "Modeling Organizational Slack: An Empirical Investigation," Stanford University Research Paper, no. 856, July 1986.

52. Ibid., p. 14.

53. Michael Schiff and Arie Y. Lewin, "The Impact of People on Budgets," *Accounting Review* (April 1970): 259–268.

54. Michael Schiff and Arie Y. Lewin, "Where Traditional Budgeting Fails," *Financial Executive* (May 1968): 51–62.

55. A. E. Lowe and R. W. Shaw, "An Analysis of Managerial Biasing: Evidence from a Company's Budgeting Process," *Journal of Management Studies* (October 1968): 304–315.

56. M. Dalton, *Men Who Manage* (New York: John Wiley and Sons, 1961), pp. 36–38.

57. G. Shillinglaw, "Divisional Performance Review: An Extension of Budgetary Control," in C. P. Bonini, R. K. Jaedicke, and H. M. Wagner, eds., *Management Controls: New Directors in Basic Research* (New York: McGraw-Hill, 1964), pp. 149–163.

58. C. Argyris, *The Impact of Budgets on People* (New York: Controllership Foundation, 1952), p. 25.

59. E. H. Caplan, *Management Accounting and Behavioral Sciences* (Reading, Mass.: Addison-Wesley, 1971).

60. Argyris, *The Impact of Budgets on People*.

61. Schiff and Lewin, "Where Traditional Budgeting Fails," pp. 51–62.

62. Mohamed Onsi, "Factor Analysis of Behavioral Variables Affecting Budgetary Slack," *Accounting Review* (July 1973): 535–548.

63. Ibid., p. 536.

64. Ibid., p. 539.

65. Ibid., p. 546.

66. Cortlandt Cammann, "Effects of the Use of Control Systems," *Accounting, Organizations and Society* (January 1976): 301–313.

67. Kenneth A. Merchant, "Budgeting and the Propensity to Create Budgetary Slack," *Accounting, Organizations and Society* (May 1985): 201–210.

68. Alan S. Dunk, "The Effect of Budget Emphasis and Information Asymmetry on the Relation between Budgetary Participation and Slack," *The Accounting Review* (April 1993): 400–410.

69. Ibid., p. 400.

70. Ibid., pp. 408–409.

71. Richard M. Cyert, J. G. March, and W. H. Starbuck, "Two Experiments on Bias and Conflict in Organizational Estimation," *Management Science* (April 1961): 254–264.

72. Lowe and Shaw, "An Analysis of Managerial Biasing."

73. Dalton, *Men Who Manage*.

74. R. M. Barefield, "A Model of Forecast Biasing Behavior," *Accounting Review* (July 1970): 490–501.

75. J. S. Demski and G. A. Feltham, "Economic Incentives in Budgetary Control Systems," *Accounting Review* (April 1978): 336–359.

76. Y. Ijiri, J. Kinard, and F. Putney, "An Integrated Evaluation System for Budget Forecasting and Operating Performance with a Classified Budgeting Bibliography," *Journal of Accounting Research* (Spring 1968): 1–28; M. Loeb and W. Magat, "Soviet Success Indicators and the Evaluation of Divisional Performance," *Journal of Accounting Research* (Spring 1978): 103–121; P. Jennergren, "On the Design of Incentives in Business Firms—A Survey of Some Research," *Management Science* (February 1980): 180–201; M. Weitzman, "The New Soviet Incentive Model," *Bell Journal of Economics* (Spring 1976): 251–257.

77. Mark S. Young, "Participative Budgeting: The Effects of Risk Aversion and Asymmetric Information on Budgetary Slack," *Journal of Accounting Research* (Autumn 1985): 829–842.

78. Ibid., pp. 831–832.

79. C. Chow, J. Cooper, and W. Waller, "Participative Budgeting: Effects of a Truth-Inducing Pay Scheme and Information Asymmetry on Slack and Performance," Working paper, University of Arizona, Tucson, 1986.

80. William S. Waller, "Slack in Participative Budgeting: The Joint Effect of a Truth-Inducing Pay Scheme and Risk Preferences," *Accounting, Organizations and Society* (December 1987): 87–98.

81. Ibid., p. 88.

82. J. Berg, L. Daley, J. Dickhaut, and J. O'Brien, "Controlling Preferences for Lotteries on Units of Experimental Exchange," *Quarterly Journal of Economics* (May 1986): 281–306.

83. D. C. Kim, "Risk Preferences in Participative Budgeting," *The Accounting Review* (April 1992): 303–318.

84. Ibid., p. 304.

85. E. Aronson and D. R. Mettee, "Dishonest Behavior as a Function of Differential Levels of Induced Self-Esteem," *Journal of Personality and Social Psychology* (January 1968): 121–127.

86. Ahmed Belkaoui, "Slack Budgeting, Information Distortion and Self-Esteem," *Contemporary Accounting Research* (Fall 1985): 111–123.

87. Kari Lukka, "Budgetary Biasing in Organizations: Theoretical Framework and Empirical Evidence," *Accounting, Organizations and Society* (February 1988): 281–301.

88. Ibid., p. 292.

89. David T. Otley, "The Accuracy of Budgetary Estimates: Some Statistical Evidence," *Journal of Business Finance and Accounting* (Fall 1985): 416.

90. W. H. Read, "Upward Communication in Industrial Hierarchies," *Human Relations* (1962): 3–16.

91. G. H. Hofstede, *The Game of Budget Control* (London: Tavistock, 1968); A. G. Hopwood, "An Empirical Study of the Role of Accounting Data in Performance Evaluation," supplement to *Journal of Accounting Research* (1972): 156–182; David T. Otley, "Budget Use and Managerial Performance," *Journal of Accounting Research* (Spring 1978): 122–149.

92. R. M. Barefield, "Comments on a Measure of Forecasting Performance," *Journal of Accounting Research* (Autumn 1969): 324–327; Otley, "The Accuracy of Budgetary Estimates."

93. G. S. Mann, "Reducing Budget Slack," *Journal of Accountancy* (August 1988): 118–122.

94. Ibid., p. 119.

95. Charles Perrow, *Complex Organizations: A Critical Essay* (Glenview, Illinois: Scott, Foreman and Company, 1972), p. 140.

SELECTED BIBLIOGRAPHY

Antle, R., and G. Eppen. "Capital Rationing and Organizational Slack in Capital Budgeting." *Management Science* (February 1985): 163–174.

Argyris, C. *The Impact of Budgets on People*. New York: Controllership Foundation, 1952.

Aronson, E., and D. R. Mettee. "Dishonest Behavior as a Function of Differential Levels of Induced Self-Esteem." *Journal of Personality and Social Psychology* (January 1968): 121–127.

Astley, W. G. "Sources of Power in Organizational Life." Ph.D. diss., University of Washington, 1978.

Barefield, R. M. "A Model of Forecast Biasing Behavior." *Accounting Review* (July 1970): 490–501.

Barnard, C. I. *Functions of the Executive*. Cambridge, Mass.: Harvard University Press, 1937.

Barnea, A., J. Ronen, and S. Sadan. "Classifactory Smoothing of Income with Extraordinary Items." *Accounting Review* (January 1976): 110–122.

Belkaoui, Ahmed. *Conceptual Foundations of Management Accounting*. Reading, Mass.: Addison-Wesley, 1980.

———. "The Relationships between Self-Disclosure Style and Attitudes to Responsibility Accounting." *Accounting, Organizations and Society* (December 1981): 281–289.

———. *Cost Accounting: A Multidimensional Emphasis*. Hinsdale, Ill.: Dryden Press, 1983.

———. "Slack Budgeting, Information Distortion and Self-Esteem." *Contemporary Accounting Research* (Fall 1985): 111–123.

Belkaoui, Ahmed, and R. D. Picur. "The Smoothing of Income Numbers: Some Empirical Evidence of Systematic Differences Between Core and Periphery Industrial Sector." *Journal of Business Finance and Accounting* (Winter 1984): 527–545.

Berg, J., L. Daley, J. Dickhaut, and J. O'Brien. "Controlling Preferences for Lotteries on Units of Experimental Exchange." *Quarterly Journal of Economics* (May 1986): 281–306.

Bonin, J. P. "On the Decision of Managerial Incentive Structures in a Decentralized Planning Environment." *American Economic Review* (September 1976): 682–687.

Bonin, J. P., and A. Marcus. "Information, Motivation, and Control in Decentralized Planning: The Case of Discretionary Managerial Behavior." *Journal of Comparative Economics* (September 1979): 235–253.

Bourgeois, L. J. "On the Measurement of Organizational Slack." *Academy of Management Review* 6, no. 1 (1981): 29–39.

Bourgeois, L. J., and W. G. Astley. "A Strategic Model of Organizational Conduct and Performance." *International Studies of Management and Organization* 9, no. 3 (1979): 40–66.

Bourgeois, L. J., and Jitendra V. Singh. "Organizational Slack and Political Behavior within Top Management Teams." Working paper, Graduate School of Business, Stanford University, 1983.

Brownell, P. "Participation in the Budgeting Process—When It Works and When It Doesn't." *Journal of Accounting Literature* (Spring 1982): 124–153.

Caplan, E. H. *Management Accounting and Behavioral Sciences*. Reading, Mass.: Addison-Wesley, 1971.

Carter, E. "The Behavioral Theory of the Firm and Top-Level Corporate Decisions." *Administrative Science Quarterly* 16, no. 4 (1971): 413–428.

Child, John. "Organizational Structure, Environment, and Performance: The Role of Strategic Choice." *Sociology* 6, no. 1 (1972): 2–22.

Chow, C., J. Cooper, and W. Waller. "Participative Budgeting: Effects of a Truth-Inducing Pay Scheme and Information Asymmetry on Slack and Performance." Working paper, University of Arizona, Tucson, 1986.

Chow, D. "The Effects of Job Standard Tightness and Compensation Scheme on Performance: An Exploration of Linkages." *Accounting Review* (October 1983): 667–685.

Christensen, J. "The Determination of Performance Standards and Participation." *Journal of Accounting Research* (Autumn 1982): 589–603.

Cohen, M. D., J. G. March, and J. P. Olsen. "A Garbage Can Model of Organizational Choice." *Administrative Science Quarterly* 17, no. 1 (1972): 1–25.

Collins, F. "Managerial Accounting Systems and Organizational Control: A Role Perspective." *Accounting, Organizations and Society* (May 1982): 107–122.

Conn, D. "A Comparison of Alternative Incentive Structures for Centrally Planned Economic Systems." *Journal of Comparative Economics* (September 1979): 261–278.

Cyert, Richard M., and James G. March. "Organizational Factors in the Theory of Oligopoly." *Quarterly Journal of Economics* (April 1956): 44–66.

————, eds. *A Behavioral Theory of the Firm*. Englewood Cliffs, N.J.: Prentice-Hall, 1963.

Cyert, Richard M., J. G. March, and W. H. Starbuck. "Two Experiments on Bias and Conflict in Organizational Estimation." *Management Science* (April 1961): 254–264.

Dalton, M. *Men Who Manage*. New York: John Wiley and Sons, 1961.

Demski, J. S., and G. A. Feltham. "Economic Incentives in Budgetary Control Systems." *Accounting Review* (April 1978): 336–359.

Dimmick, D. E., and V. V. Murray. "Correlates of Substantive Policy Decisions in Organizations: The Case of Human Resource Management." *Academy of Management Journal* 21, no. 4 (1978): 611–623.

Dunk, Alan S. "The Effect of Budget Emphasis and Information Asymmetry on the Relation Between Budgetary Participation and Slack." *The Accounting Review* (April 1993): 400–410.

Fitts, W. F. *Manual for the Tennessee Self-Concept Scale*. Nashville, Tenn.: Counselor Recording and Tests, 1965.

————. *Interpersonal Competence: The Wheel Model*. Nashville, Tenn.: Counselor Recording and Tests, 1970.

————. *The Self-Concept and Behavior: Overview and Supplement*. Nashville, Tenn.: Counselor Recordings and Tests, 1972.

————. *The Self-Concept and Performance*. Nashville, Tenn.: Counselor Recording and Tests, 1972.

————. *The Self-Concept and Psychopathology*. Nashville, Tenn.: Counselor Recording and Tests, 1972.

Fitts, W. F., J. L. Adams, G. Radford, W. C. Richard, B. K. Thomas, M. M. Thomas, and W. Thompson. *The Self-Concept and Self-Actualization*. Nashville, Tenn.: Counselor Recording and Tests, 1971.

Fitts, W. F., and W. T. Hammer. *The Self-Concept and Delinquency*. Nashville, Tenn.: Counselor Recording and Tests, 1969.

Galbraith, Jay. *Designing Complex Organizations*. Reading, Mass.: Addison-Wesley, 1973.

Gonik, J. "Tie Salesmen's Bonuses to Their Forecasts." *Harvard Business Review* (May-June 1978): 116–123.

Gordon, M. J., B. N. Horwitz, and P. T. Myers. "Accounting Measurements and Normal Growth of the Firm." In R. K. Jaedicke, Y. Ijiri, and O. Nieslen, eds., *Research in Accounting Measurement*. Sarasota, Fla.: American Accounting Association, 1966.

Hambrick, D. C., and C. C. Snow. "A Contextual Model of Strategic Decision Making in Organizations." In R. L. Taylor, J. J. O'Connell, R. A. Zawacki, and D. D. Warrick, eds., *Academy of Management Proceedings* (1977): 109–112.

Hershey, J., H. Kunreuther, and P. Shoemaker. "Bias in Assessment Procedures for Utility Functions." *Management Science* (August 1982): 936–954.

Hopwood, A. G. "An Empirical Study of the Role of Accounting Data in Performance Evaluation." *Journal of Accounting Research* (supplement, 1972): 156–182.

Ijiri, Y., J. Kinard, and F. Putney. "An Integrated Evaluation System for Budget Forecasting and Operating Performance with a Classified Budgeting Bibliography." *Journal of Accounting Research* (Spring 1968): 1–28.

Itami, H. "Evaluation Measures and Goal Congruence under Uncertainty." *Journal of Accounting Research* (Spring 1975): 163–180.

Jennergren, P. "On the Design of Incentives in Business Firms—A Survey of Some Research." *Management Science* (February 1980): 180–201.

Kamin, J. Y., and J. Ronen. "The Smoothing of Income Numbers: Some Empirical Evidence on Systematic Differences among Management-Controlled and Owner-Controlled Firms." *Accounting, Organizations and Society* (October 1978): 141–157.

Kerr, S., and W. Slocum, Jr. "Controlling the Performances of People in Organizations." In W. Starbuck and P. Nystrom, eds., *Handbook of Organizational Design*, Vol. 2, 116–134. New York: Oxford University Press, 1981.

Kim, D. C. "Risk Preferences in Participative Budgeting." *The Accounting Review* (April 1992): 303–319.

Lecky, P. *Self-Consistency*. New York: Island Press, 1945.

Leibenstein, Harvey. "Allocative Efficiency vs. 'X-Efficiency.'" *American Economic Review* (June 1966): 392–415.

———. "X-Efficiency: From Concept to Theory." *Challenge* (September-October 1979): 13–22.

Levinthal, D., and J. G. March. "A Model of Adaptive Organizational Search." *Journal of Economic Behavior and Organization* (May 1981): 307–333.

Lewin, Arie Y., and Carl Wolf. "The Theory of Organizational Slack: A Critical Review." *Proceedings: Twentieth International Meeting of TIMS* (1976): 648–654.

———. "Organizational Slack: A Test of the General Theory." *Journal of Management Studies* (forthcoming).

Litschert, R. J., and T. W. Bonham. "A Conceptual Model of Strategy Formation." *Academy of Management Review* 3, no. 2 (1978): 211–219.

Locke, E., and D. Schweiger. "Participation in Decision Making: One More Look." In B. Staw, ed., *Research in Organizational Behavior*, 265–339. Greenwich, Conn.: JAI Press, 1979.

Loeb, M., and W. Magat. "Soviet Success Indicators and the Evaluation of Divisional Performance." *Journal of Accounting Research* (Spring 1978): 103–121.

Lowe, A. E., and R. W. Shaw. "An Analysis of Managerial Biasing: Evidence from a Company's Budgeting Process." *Journal of Management Studies* (October 1968): 304–315.

March, James G. Interview by Stanford Business School Alumni Association, *Stanford GSB* 47, no. 3 (1978–1979): 16–19.

———. "Decisions in Organizations and Theories of Choice." In Andrew H. Van de Ven and William F. Joyce, eds., *Perspectives on Organizational Design and Behavior*, 215–235. New York: John Wiley and Sons, 1981.

March, James G., and H. A. Simon. *Organizations*. New York: John Wiley and Sons, 1958.

Merchant, Kenneth A. "The Design of the Corporate Budgeting System: Influences on Managerial Behavior and Performance." *Accounting Review* (October 1981): 813–829.

Mezias, Stephen J. "Some Analytics of Organizational Slack." Working paper, Graduate School of Business, Stanford University, November 1985.

Miller, J., and J. Thornton. "Effort, Uncertainty, and the New Soviet Incentive System." *Southern Economic Journal* (October 1978): 432–446.

Mitroff, I. I., and J. R. Emshoff. "On Strategic Assumption-Making: A Dialectical Approach to Policy and Planning." *Academy of Management Review* 4, no. 1 (1979): 1–12.

Moch, M. K., and L. R. Pondy. "The Structure of Chaos: Organized Anarchy as a Response to Ambiguity." *Administrative Science Quarterly* 22, no. 2 (1977): 351–362.

Onsi, Mohamed. "Factor Analysis of Behavioral Variables Affecting Budgetary Slack." *Accounting Review* (July 1973): 535–548.

Parker, L. D. "Goal Congruence: A Misguided Accounting Concept." *ABACUS* (June 1976): 3–13.

Pondy, L. R. "Organizational Conflict: Concepts and Models." *Administrative Science Quarterly* 12, no. 2 (1967): 296–320.

Radner, R. "A Behavioral Model of Cost Reduction." *Bell Journal of Economics* (Fall 1975): 196–215.

Rogers, C. R. *Client Centered Therapy*. Boston: Houghton Mifflin, 1951.

Rosner, Martin M. "Economic Determinant of Organizational Innovation." *Administrative Science Quarterly* 12 (1968): 614–625.

Schein, V. E. "Examining an Illusion: The Role of Deceptive Behaviors in Organizations." *Human Relations* (October 1979): 287–295.

Schiff, Michael. "Accounting Tactics and the Theory of the Firm." *Journal of Accounting Research* (Spring 1966): 62–67.

Schiff, Michael, and Arie Y. Levin. "Where Traditional Budgeting Fails." *Financial Executive* (May 1968): 51–62.

———. "The Impact of People on Budgets." *Accounting Review* (April 1970): 259–268.

———. *Behavioral Aspects of Accounting*. Englewood Cliffs, N.J.: Prentice-Hall, 1974.

Simon, H. A. *Administrative Behavior*. New York: Free Press, 1957.

Singh, Jitendra V. "Performance, Slack, and Risk Taking in Strategic Decisions: Test of a Structural Equation Model." Ph.D. Diss., Stanford Graduate School of Business, 1983.

———. "Performance, Slack, and Risk Taking in Organizational Decision Making." *Academy of Management Journal* (September 1986): 562–585.

Snowberger, V. "The New Soviet Incentive Model: Comment." *Bell Journal of Economics* (Autumn 1977): 591–600.

Snygg, D., and A. W. Combs. *Individual Behavior*. New York: Harper and Row, 1949.

Staw, B. M. "Rationality and Justification in Organizational Life." In B. M. Staw and L. L. Cummings, eds., *Research in Organizational Behavior*, Vol. 2, 154–82. Greenwich, Conn.: JAI Press, 1980.

Swieringa, R. J., and R. H. Moncur. "The Relationship between Managers' Budget Oriented Behavior and Selected Attitudes, Position, Size and Performance Measures." *Journal of Accounting Research* (supplement, 1972): 19.

Thompson, J. D. *Organizations in Action*. New York: McGraw-Hill, 1967.

Thompson, W. *Correlates of the Self-Concept*. Nashville, Tenn.: Counselor Recording and Tests, 1972.

Waller, William S. "Slack in Participative Budgeting: The Joint Effect of a Truth-Inducing Pay Scheme and Risk Preferences." *Accounting, Organizations and Society* (December 1987): 87–98.

Waller, William S., and C. Chow. "The Self-Selection and Effort of Standard-Based Employment Contracts: A Framework and Some Empirical Evidence." *Accounting Review* (July 1985): 458–476.

Weitzman, M. "The New Soviet Incentive Model." *Bell Journal of Economics* (Spring 1976): 251–257.

Williamson, Oliver E. "A Model of Rational Managerial Behavior." In Richard M. Cyert and James G. March, eds., *A Behavioral Theory of the Firm*, 113–128. Englewood Cliffs, N.J.: Prentice-Hall, 1963.

————. *The Economics of Discretionary Behavior: Managerial Objectives in a Theory of the Firm*. Englewood Cliffs, N.J.: Prentice-Hall, 1964.

Winter, Sidney G. "Satisficing, Selection, and the Innovating Remnant." *Quarterly Journal of Economics* 85 (1971): 237–257.

Woot, P. D., H. Heyvaert, and F. Martou. "Strategic Management: An Empirical Study of 168 Belgian Firms." *International Studies of Management and Organization* 7 (1977): 60–73.

Wylie, R. C. *The Self-Concept: A Critical Survey of Pertinent Research Literature*. Lincoln: University of Nebraska Press, 1961.

Young, Mark S. "Participative Budgeting: The Effects of Risk Aversion and Asymmetric Information on Budgetary Slack." *Journal of Accounting Research* (Autumn 1985): 829–842.

2

Properties of Organizational Slack in the U.S. Context

2.1 THE ANALYSIS OF THE PROPERTIES OF ORGANIZATIONAL SLACK

The accounting literature has actively examined the question of how various groupings of firms differ or are similar in terms of financial characteristics. Such groupings or classifications include industry membership,[1] size, similarity of accounting and/or market-based variables,[2] fiscal year-end, and/or stock exchange membership.[3] The presence of systematic financial differences among groupings creates difficulties in interpreting empirical research findings. For example, unexpected security price changes and duration of price adjustments were found to be sensitive to certain financial characteristics, such as firm size, that differ systematically between subgroups of companies.[4]

Most empirical research relying on financial data fail to examine the properties of organizational slack measures and the question of how various groupings of firms differ or are similar in terms of organizational slack measures. The differences of firms in terms of type of membership in stock exchange, fiscal year ending, and membership in economic sectors leads to differences in organizational slack. In addition, the profitability of firms is related to their organizational slack strategies. Accordingly, this chapter examines the following two research questions: (1) Does the differences of U.S. firms in terms of type of membership in stock exchanges, fiscal year ending, and membership in economic sectors lead to differences in organizational slack?, and (2) Is the level and variance in the profitability of U.S. firms related to the level and variance in organizational slack?

Three measures of organizational slack are used in this study. They are defined as follows:

1. *administrative slack* = general and administrative expenses/cost of
       goods sold

This is the proportion of general and administrative costs relative to cost of
goods sold. It points to the creation of organizational slack via an increase in the
staff or administrative component. This concept of slack as extra staff, as suggested by Williamson,[5] has also been used by Bourgeois and Singh[6] and Singh.[7]

2. *available liquidity* = (cash + marketable securities – current
       liabilities)/sales

This concept measures the most liquid current assets relative to current liabilities.
It points to the creation of organizational slack via an increase in readily accessible
liquid resources not absorbed by costs. This concept of slack as available and readily accessible liquid resources has been used by Singh[8] and Bourgeois and Singh.[9]

3. *recoverable liquidity* = (accounts receivable + inventory)/sales

This concept measures the potential but not yet realized revenues. It points to
the creation of organizational slack via an increase in realizable revenues in the
form of credit sales and potential sales that will be converted to cash in the future. This concept of slack as recoverable liquidity has been used by Bourgeois
and Singh.[10]

2.2 SAMPLE OF U.S. COMPANIES

The sample of companies used for this study included 2544 companies from
394 four-digit Standard Industry Classification (SIC) industries. The period of
analysis covered the 1985–1991 period.

2.3 DETERMINANTS OF DIFFERENCES IN
ORGANIZATIONAL SLACK

This section examines the question of how various groupings of U.S. firms differ or are similar in terms of organizational slack. These groupings include the
type of membership in stock exchanges, the type of fiscal year ending (December versus non-December ending), and the influence of core versus periphery
sectors membership.

2.4 INFLUENCE OF THE TYPE OF MEMBERSHIP IN
STOCK EXCHANGES

Four categories are used to identify the major exchanges on which the companies' common stocks are traded. They are as follows:

SE_1 = New York Stock Exchange

SE_2 = American Stock Exchange

SE_3 = Over-the-Counter Market

SE_4 = Canadian and Regional Exchanges

Exhibit 2.1 summarizes the univariate statistical characteristics for each organizational slack variable by stock exchange type for the 1986–1991 period. The analyses of variance results are summarized in Exhibit 2.2 for administrative slack, Exhibit 2.3 for available liquidity, and Exhibit 2.4 for recoverable liquidity. The comparison of means results are shown in Exhibit 2.5 for administrative slack, Exhibit 2.6 for available liquidity and Exhibit 2.7 for recoverable liquidity.

The results for administrative slack show that this measure of slack is the highest for firms listed in the American Stock Exchange. The lowest value is for firms listed in Canadian and regional exchanges. The analysis of variance results show also that the type of stock exchange on which the companies' common stocks are traded has a significant impact on the level of administrative slack relied on by U.S. firms.

The results for available liquidity show that this measure of organizational slack is also the highest for firms listed on the American Stock Exchange. The lowest value is still for firms listed in Canadian and regional stock exchanges. The analysis of variance results show also that the type of stock exchange on which the companies' common stocks are traded has a significant impact on the level of available liquidity relied on by U.S. firms.

Finally, the results for recoverable liquidity show that this measure of slack is still the highest for firms listed in the American Stock Exchange. The lowest value is for firms listed in over-the-counter market. The analysis of variance results also show that the type of stock exchange on which the companies' common stocks are listed and traded has a significant impact on the level of recoverable liquidity created by U.S. firms.

The influence of the type of stock exchanges on all types of organizational slacks created by U.S. firms is highly significant, with firms listed on the American Stock Exchanges exhibiting the highest levels.

2.5 INFLUENCE OF THE TYPE OF FISCAL YEAR ENDING

Two categories are used to identify the type of fiscal year ending: December ending or non-December ending.

Exhibit 2.8 summarizes the univariate statistical characteristics for each organizational slack variable by type of fiscal year ending for the 1986–1991 period. The analyses of variance results are summarized in Exhibit 2.9 for administrative slack, in Exhibit 2.10 for available liquidity, and in Exhibit 2.11 for recoverable liquidity.

Exhibit 2.1
Univariate Characteristics by Stock Exchange Type

Administrative Slack

Stock Exchange (SE)	Size	Mean	Standard Deviation	Skewness	Kurtosis	T: Mean = 0
SE_1	7354	0.4353	0.7268	12.7078	255.0537	51.3657*
SE_2	3570	0.5795	1.1451	8.1517	93.0941	30.2415*
SE_3	-	-	-	-	-	-
SE_4	217	0.2253	0.20107	1.9230	3.4749	16.5089*

Available Liquidity

Stock Exchange (SE)	Size	Mean	Standard Deviation	Skewness	Kurtosis	T: Mean = 0
SE_1	10416	-0.0509	0.7455	-1.303	117.7876	-6.9695*
SE_2	4435	0.0720	1.3525	4.4163	58.8409	3.5486*
SE_3	35	-0.1084	0.8221	-1.9747	6.3207	-0.7803
SE_4	331	-0.2184	0.4619	-5.1866	44.8535	-8.6011*

Recoverable Liquidity

Stock Exchange (SE)	Size	Mean	Standard Deviation	Skewness	Kurtosis	T: Mean = 0
SE_1	8793	0.5018	1.1033	6.8594	55.8277	42.6464*
SE_2	4156	0.5772	1.3733	6.3914	46.6852	27.0975*
SE_3	15	0.2040	0.1065	-0.0863	-1.0010	7.4138*
SE_4	222	0.2867	0.1377	1.3486	2.8455	31.0205*

SE_1 = New York Stock Exchange SE_3 = Over-the-Counter
SE_2 = American Stock Exchange SE_4 = Canadian and Regional Exchanges
° = Significant at $\alpha = 0.01$

Exhibit 2.2
Analysis of Variance: Effects of Stock Exchange Membership on Administrative Slack

Source	DF	Sum of Squares	Mean Square	F Value	Pr > F
Stock Exchange Membership	2	64.0529	32.0264	41.61	0.0001
Error	11138	8573.4056	0.7697		
Total	11140	8637.4585			

Exhibit 2.3
Analysis of Variance: Effects of Stock Exchange Membership on Available Liquidity

Source	DF	Sum of Squares	Mean Square	F Value	Pr > F
Stock Exchange Membership	3	60.8350	20.2783	22.04	0.0001
Error	15213	13994.3703	0.91989		
Total	15216	14055.2053			

Exhibit 2.4
Analysis of Variance: Effects of Stock Exchange Membership on Recoverable Liquidity

Source	DF	Sum of Squares	Mean Square	F Value	Pr > F
Stock Exchange Membership	3	30.0829	10.0276	7.13	0.0001
Error	13182	18544.3057	1.40679		
Total	13185				

The results for administrative slack show that this measure of slack is highest for "non-December" firms. The analysis of variance results show that the type of fiscal year ending has a significant impact on the level of administrative slack created by U.S. firms.

Exhibit 2.5
Comparison of Means: Effects of Stock Exchange Membership on Administrative Slack

Stock Exchange	Lower Confidence Limit	Difference Between Means	Upper Confidence Limit
$SE_2 - SE_1$	0.10913	0.14421	0.17929*
$SE_2 - SE_4$	0.23400	0.35424	0.47448*
$SE_1 - SE_2$	-0.17929	-0.14421	-0.10913*
$SE_1 - SE_4$	0.09158	0.21003	0.32849*
$SE_4 - SE_2$	-0.47448	-0.35424	-0.23400*
$SE_4 - SE_1$	-0.32849	-0.21003	-0.09158*

SE_1 = New York Stock Exchange
SE_2 = American Stock Exchange
SE_3 = Over-the-Counter
SE_4 = Canadian and Regional Exchanges
° = Significant at $\alpha = 0.05$

The results for both available and recoverable liquidity show that these two measures of organizational slack are the highest for "December" firms. In addition, the analysis of variance results show that the type of fiscal year ending has a significant impact on the levels of available liquidity and recoverable liquidity.

2.6 INFLUENCE OF CORE VERSUS PERIPHERY SECTORS MEMBERSHIP

2.6.1 Stratification in a Dual Economy

Models of sectoral differentiation derived from theories of economic dualism exhibit three main perspectives: (1) theories of a dual economy, (2) dual labor markets, and (3) labor force segmentation.[11,12,13] A common characteristic of these three perspectives is the division of the industrial structure of the economy into two distinct sectors (at least in the two-sector model) consisting of the *core* and *periphery* sectors. These models, however, present different definitions and conceptualizations of these sectors.

The dual labor market and labor force segmentation literature defines the sectors or segments in terms of the characteristics of labor markets and worker behavior.[14,15] Common to both perspectives is the argument that, corresponding

Exhibit 2.6
Comparison of Means: Effects of Stock Exchange Membership on Available Liquidity

Stock Exchange	Lower Confidence Limit	Difference Between Means	Upper Confidence Limit
$SE_2 - SE_1$	0.08928	0.12299	0.15669*
$SE_2 - SE_3$	-0.13851	0.18051	0.49954*
$SE_2 - SE_4$	0.18336	0.29048	0.39760*
$SE_1 - SE_2$	-0.15669	-0.12299	-0.08928*
$SE_1 - SE_3$	-0.26078	0.05753	0.37583*
$SE_1 - SE_4$	0.06253	0.16749	0.27246*
$SE_3 - SE_2$	-0.49954	-0.18051	0.13851*
$SE_3 - SE_1$	-0.37583	-0.05753	0.26078*
$SE_3 - SE_4$	-0.22419	0.10997	0.44412*
$SE_4 - SE_2$	-0.39760	-0.29048	-0.18336*
$SE_4 - SE_1$	-0.27246	-0.16749	-0.06253*
$SE_4 - SE_3$	-0.44412	-0.10997	0.22419

SE_1 = New York Stock Exchange
SE_2 = American Stock Exchange
SE_3 = Over-the-Counter
SE_4 = Canadian and Regional Exchanges
° = Significant at $\alpha = 0.05$

to the core and periphery sectors, respectively, there are two separate labor markets: a primary labor market and a secondary labor market, distinguished by the extent to which employment is relatively stable and secure. For example, M. Piore defines the two sectors as follows:

> The central tenet of the analysis is that the role of employment and of the disposition of manpower in the perpetuation of poverty is best understood in terms of a dual labor market. One sector of the market, which I have termed elsewhere the primary market, offers jobs which possess several of the following traits: high wages, good working conditions, employment stability and job security, equity and due process in the administration of work rules, and chances for advancement. The other, or secondary market, has jobs which, relative to those in the primary sector, are decidedly less

Exhibit 2.7
Comparison of Means: Effects of Stock Exchange Membership on Recoverable Liquidity

Stock Exchange	Lower Confidence Limit	Difference Between Means	Upper Confidence Limit
$SE_2 - SE_1$	0.03170	0.07546	0.11922*
$SE_2 - SE_4$	0.13039	0.29054	0.45069*
$SE_2 - SE_3$	-0.22813	0.37323	0.97460*
$SE_1 - SE_2$	-0.11922	-0.07546	-0.03170*
$SE_1 - SE_4$	0.05709	0.21508	0.37308*
$SE_1 - SE_3$	-0.30302	0.29777	0.89857*
$SE_4 - SE_2$	-0.45069	-0.29054	-0.13039*
$SE_4 - SE_1$	-0.37308	-0.21508	-0.05709*
$SE_4 - SE_3$	-0.53754	0.08269	0.70292
$SE_3 - SE_2$	-0.97460	-0.37323	0.22813
$SE_3 - SE_1$	-0.89857	-0.29777	0.30302
$SE_3 - SE_4$	-0.70292	-0.08269	0.53754

° = Significant at $\alpha = 0.05$

attractive. They tend to involve low wages, poor working conditions, considerable variability in employment, harsh and often arbitrary discipline, and little opportunity to advance. The poor are confined to the secondary labor market. The elimination of poverty requires that they gain access to primary employment.[16]

The dual economy perspective, as illustrated by writers such as R. T. Averitt[17] and B. Bluestone et al.,[18] views the economic sectors as structural entities derived from the nature of modern industrial capitalism. It is often argued that sector differentiation resulted from the creation during the late nineteenth and early twentieth centuries of a core industrial sector dominated by large oligopolistic corporations.[19] For example, Averitt characterizes the two sectors as follows:

The new economy is composed of firms large in size and influence. Its organizations are corporate and bureaucratic; its production processes are

Exhibit 2.8
Univariate Characteristics by Fiscal Year

Administrative Slack

Fiscal Year	Size	Mean	Standard Deviation	Skewness	Kurtosis	T: Mean = 0
Non-December	4743	0.5414	0.9814	8.9708	115.949	37.992*
December	6605	0.4497	0.8350	11.144	191.055	43.776*

Available Liquidity

Fiscal Year	Size	Mean	Standard Deviation	Skewness	Kurtosis	T: Mean = 0
Non-December	5526	-0.0392	0.9014	6.1970	99.177	-3.2327*
December	10684	0.0409	0.9868	1.8700	91.183	4.2961*

Recoverable Liquidity

Fiscal Year	Size	Mean	Standard Deviation	Skewness	Kurtosis	T: Mean = 0
Non-December	5222	0.4508	0.8903	8.8772	97.9821	36.5930*
December	8275	0.5578	1.3213	6.1329	43.4019	38.4045*

° = Significant at $\alpha = 0.05$

vertically integrated through ownership and control of critical raw material supplies and product distributions; its activities are diversified into many industries, regions, and nations. . . . Firms in the large economy serve national and international markets, using technologically progressive systems of production and distribution. . . . We shall call this network of firms the "center."

The other economy is populated by relatively small firms. These enterprises are the ones usually dominated by a single individual or family. The firm's sales are realized in restricted markets. . . . Techniques of production and marketing are rarely up to date as those in the center. . . . Let us designate the firms in the small economy by the term "periphery."[20]

Exhibit 2.9
Analysis of Variance: Effects of Fiscal Year Ending on Administrative Slack

Source	DF	Sum of Squares	Mean Square	F. Value	Pr > F
Fiscal Year Ending	1	23.1767	23.1767	28.67	0.0001
Error	11346	9172.2922	0.8084		
Total	11347	9195.4689			

Bluestone et al. provides a similar characterization as follows:

> The core economy includes those industries that comprise the muscle of American economic and political power. . . . Entrenched in durable manufacturing, the construction of trades and, to a lesser extent, the extraction industries, the firms in the core economy are noted for high productivity, high profits, intensive utilization of capital, high incidence of monopoly elements, and a high degree of unionization. What follows normally from such characteristics are high wages. The automobile, steel, rubber, aluminum, aerospace, and petroleum industries are ranking members of this part of the economy. Workers who are able to secure employment in those industries are in most cases, assured of relatively higher wages and better than average working conditions and fringe benefits.[21]

The basic distinction in the dual economy perspective is made in terms of market power, with the core industries characterized as monopolists or oligopolists, and periphery firms as competitors. Other distinctions include financial size, scale of employment, conglomerate organization, long-term planning capabilities, and relationship to government.[22] The relationship between the two sec-

Exhibit 2.10
Analysis of Variance: Effects of Fiscal Year Ending on Available Liquidity

Source	DF	Sum of Squares	Mean Square	F. Value	Pr > F
Fiscal Year Ending	1	23.4123	23.4123	25.48	0.0001
Error	16208	14892.9095	0.9188		
Total	16209	14916.3219			

Exhibit 2.11
Analysis of Variance: Effects of Fiscal Year Ending on Recoverable Liquidity

Source	DF	Sum of Squares	Mean Square	F. Value	Pr > F
Fiscal Year Ending	1	36.6338	36.6338	26.60	0.0001
Error	13495	18585.3040	1.3771		
Total	13496	18621.9379		.	

tors is assumed to be one of dependency, with core firms extracting monopoly profits from the periphery firms to which they sell, demanding "preferred" customer rebates from their suppliers, and the periphery firms existing as satellites of core firms or customers.[23] What it implies is that beyond the fringes of the core economy lie a set of industries that lack almost all the advantages normally found in the core firms. Concentrated in agriculture, nondurable manufacturing, retail trade, and subprofessional services, the periphery industries are noted for their small firm size, labor intensity, low profits, low productivity, intensive product market competition, lack of unionization, and low wages. Unlike core firms, the firms in the periphery sector lack the assets, size, and political power to take advantage of economies of scale or spend large sums on research and development.

2.6.2 Related Research

The early literature on dualism was descriptive, focusing on proper definitions of the two sectors as core versus periphery,[24] concentrated versus unconcentrated,[25] monopoly versus competitive,[26] and planned versus market economies.[27] What followed were empirical attempts at understanding the differences between the two sectors using factor analysis and cluster analysis.[28]

The basic purpose of empirical research on dualism is to differentiate economic units categorized in a monopoly/core sector versus a competitive/periphery sector on the basis of empirical measures. The earlier attempts to operationalize industry segments by R. Bibbs and W. Form[29] and E. M. Beck et al.[30] relied on the narrative description of major industrial sectors as periphery or core sectors by Averitt[31] or the same description by Bluestone et al.[32] These early studies were followed by empirical attempts to define industrial sectors by using either a factor analysis of economic and structural data as in the studies by R. Hodson,[33] G. Oster,[34] and C. Tolbert et al.[35] or a factor analysis followed by cluster analysis. Hodson,[36] Oster,[37] and Tolbert[38] were able to identify two sectors. All these studies used the industry rather than the firm as the unit of analysis, arguing that firms in industries are similar in technologies and organizational forms and face similar variations in the demands for their products. In addition, these studies relied on macroeconomic and industry-based variables and data.

2.6.3 Models for Classifying Firms into the Economic Sectors

Because there is no single theory of the dual economy, it is not possible to operationalize the concept to develop a unique classification of "core" versus "periphery" firms. In most studies, firms are grouped into either a core or a periphery sector, based on a sectorial classification provided by Beck et al.[39] and illustrated in Exhibit 2.12. The choice of this core versus periphery industry classification is based on the timeliness relative to the fairly similar classifications of Bibbs and Form,[40] the ease of operationalizing industry classes into firm specific ones, and their acceptance in the economic literature.[41]

Philip Karpik and Ahmed Riahi-Belkaoui[42] used instead a logistic regression to test the significance of a model explaining the core/periphery classification as a function of a set of financial characteristics or ratios. The logistic regression model of the following form was estimated:[43]

$$\ln (P_{cs}/1 - P_{cs}) = b_0 + b_1\text{BE} + b_2\text{TA} + b_3\text{CR} + b_4\text{DLTA} + b_5\text{FCR} + b_6\text{PE} + b_7\text{CIS}$$

where

b_j	=	regression coefficients
BE	=	beta (equal weighted index [annual returns] in the market model)
TA	=	Total assets
CR	=	Current ratio
DLTA	=	Long Term Debt/Total Assets
FCR	=	Fixed Coverage Ratio
PE	=	Price Earnings Ratio
CIS	=	Gross Plant/Sales.

Exhibit 2.13 presents the results of the logistic model using the complete sample of firms in the core and periphery sectors for 1988.[44] The overall model was significant at alpha <0.001. Six of the seven variables had coefficients of the expected sign and significance levels at alpha <0.05. These coefficients are consistent with periphery firms being riskier, having lower current ratios, decreased levels of capital intensity, while having greater leverage and higher levels of fixed charge coverage. Only size as measured by total assets (TA), was not significant, although the negative coefficient is consistent with periphery firms being smaller than core firms.[45]

The Karpik-Belkaoui model, as shown in Exhibit 2.12, was used in this study to classify firms into either a core or periphery sector.

Exhibit 2.12
Sectoral Classifications

Industry Group	Sector
Agriculture, forestry and fisheries	Periphery
Mining	
Metal mining	Core
Coal mining	Core
Crude Petroleum and natural gas	Core
Nonmetallic mining and quarrying	Core
Construction	Core
Durable Manufacturing	
Lumber and wood products	Periphery
Furniture and fixtures	Periphery
Stone, clay, and glass products	Core
Metal industries	Core
Machinery, except electrical	Core
Electrical machinery, equipment, supplies	Core
Transportation equipment	Core
Professional and photographic equipment	Core
Ordnance	Core
Miscellaneous durable manufacturing	Periphery
Nondurable Manufacturing	
Food and kindred products	Periphery
Tobacco Manufacturers	Periphery
Textile mill products	Periphery
Apparel and other fabricated textiles	Periphery
Paper and allied products	Core
Printing, publishing and allied industries	Core
Chemical and allied products	Core
Petroleum and coal products	Core
Rubber and miscellaneous plastic products	Core
Leather and leather products	Periphery
Not specified nondurable manufacturing	Periphery
Transportation	
Railroads and railway express service	Core
Street railways and bus lines	Core
Taxicab service	Core
Trucking service	Core
Warehousing and storage	Core
Water transportation	Core
Petroleum and gasoline pipelines	Core
Services incidental to transportation	Core
Communications	
Radio broadcasting and television	Core
Telephone (wire and radio)	Core

(continued)

Exhibit 2.12   (Continued)

Industry Group	Sector
Telegraph (wire and radio)	Core
Utilities and sanitary services	
Electric light and power	Core
Gas, steam and supply systems	Core
Electric-gas utilities	Core
Water supply	Core
Sanitation services	Core
Other not specified utilities	Core
Wholesale trade	Core
Retail trade	Periphery
Finance, insurance, and real estate	Core
Business and repair services	Periphery
Personal services	Periphery
Entertainment and recreation services	Periphery
Professional and related services	Core
Public administration	Core

2.6.4 Results of the Influence of Economic Sector Classification on Organizational Slack

Exhibit 2.14 summarizes the univariate statistical characteristics for each organizational slack variable by type of economic sector classification, core versus periphery, for the 1986–1991 period. The analyses of variance results are summarized in Exhibit 2.15 for administrative slack, Exhibit 2.16 for available liquidity, and Exhibit 2.17 for recoverable liquidity.

The results of the analyses of variance show that the economic sector classification into core or periphery sectors has a significant impact on the three measures of organizational slack. *Basically, administrative slack, available liquidity, and recoverable liquidity are higher for firms in the periphery sector than in the core sector.*

2.7 EFFECTS OF ORGANIZATIONAL SLACK POLICIES ON THE LEVEL AND VARIANCE OF PROFITABILITY

2.7.1 The Objective Function in Management Accounting

Many authors in the field of complex organizations define an organization as a social system that is created to achieve certain specific goals or objectives. For example, Amitai Etzioni defines organizations as "social units (or human groupings) deliberately constructed and reconstructed to seek specific goals."[46] Richard Hall states: "An organization is a collectivity with a relatively identifiable boundary, a normative order, authority ranks, community systems, and membership coordinating systems; this collectivity exists on a relatively continuous

Exhibit 2.13
Logistic Model of Dual Economy Classes: Data for 1988 (N = 1,423)

```
Dependent variable (Dual) = 0 if core (N = 1,257), and

                           1 if periphery class (n = 167).


Model chi-square statistic = 72.96 with d.f. = 7;

        Probability under H_0 < .00001.



     Model Parameters: Independent Variable* Coefficients
```

| | Expected | Coef. | | | |
Variable	Sign	Beta	Std. Error	Chi-Square	Prob. <
Intercept	?	−1.23846	0.31144	15.81	.0001
BETA_E	+	+0.14140	0.06132	5.32	.0211
TA_5	−	−0.00004	0.00005	0.61	.4347
CR_5	−	−0.53702	0.11459	21.96	.0001
DLTA_5	+	1.66442	0.45076	13.63	.0002
FCR_5	+	0.09031	0.02576	12.29	.0005
PE_5	+	0.02213	0.00886	6.24	.0125
CIS_5	−	−1.29823	0.24480	28.12	.0001

*Independent variables were truncated using a 5 percent filter, except for Beta which is already adjusted (normalized to the population mean), to reduce departures from normality.

basis in an environment and engages in activities that are usually related to a goal or a set of goals."[47]

The concept of organizational goal and/or objective has not, however, been clearly defined in the literature. The general goals refer to the intentions or wishes espoused by those persons who develop them. For example, V. Buck gives the following operational definition of organizational goals: "It is the decision to commit resources for certain activities and to withhold them from certain others that operationally defines the organization's goals. Verbal pronouncements are insufficient for defining goals; the speaker must put his resources where his mouth is if something is to be considered a goal."[48]

Different typologies of goals have also been proposed. First, J. D. Thompson differentiated between goals held for an organization and goals of an organization.[49] The former are held by persons who are not members of the organization

Exhibit 2.14
Univariate Characteristics by Economic Sectors

A. Administrative Slack

Economic Sector	Size	Mean	Standard Deviation	Skewness	Kurtosis	T: Mean = 0
Core Sector	7354	0.4353	0.7268	12.7078	255.0537	51.3657*
Periphery Sector	3787	0.5592	1.1158	8.3555	98.0529	30.8433*

B. Available Liquidity

Economic Sector	Size	Mean	Standard Deviation	Skewness	Kurtosis	T: Mean = 0
Core Sector	10416	-0.0509	0.7455	-1.303	117.7876	-6.9695*
Periphery Sector	4801	0.0507	1.3095	4.5170	62.3676	2.6841*

C. Recoverable Liquidity

Economic Sector	Size	Mean	Standard Deviation	Skewness	Kurtosis	T: Mean = 0
Core Sector	8793	0.5018	1.1033	6.8594	55.8277	42.6464*
Periphery Sector	4393	0.5613	1.3378	6.5758	49.5078	27.8085*

° Significant at $\alpha = 0.05$

but have a given interest in the activities of the firm, such as clientele, investors, action groups, and so on. The latter are held by persons who are part of the "dominant coalition" in terms of holding enough control to commit the organization to a given direction.

C. Perrow made a distinction between "official goals" and "operative goals."[50] Official goals refer to those objectives or general purposes stated either orally or in writing by key members. Operative goals refer to the designated objectives based on the actual operating policies of the organization. Etzioni refers to such goals as real goals. They constitute "the future states toward which a majority of

Exhibit 2.15
Analysis of Variance: Effects of Economic Sectors on Administrative Slack

Source	DF	Sum of Squares	Mean Square	F Value	Pr > F
Economic Sector	1	38.3822	38.3822	49.72	0.0001
Error	11139	8599.0762	0.77197		
Total	11140	8637.4585			

Exhibit 2.16
Analysis of Variance: Effects of Economic Sectors on Available Liquidity

Source	DF	Sum of Squares	Mean Square	F Value	Pr > F
Economic Sector	1	33.9520	33.9520	36.84	0.0001
Error	15215	14021.2533	0.9215		
Total	15216	14055.2053			

Exhibit 2.17
Analysis of Variance: Effects of Economic Sectors on Recoverable Liquidity

Source	DF	Sum of Squares	Mean Square	F Value	Pr > F
Economic Sector	1	10.3718	10.3178	7.37	0.0067
Error	13184	18564.0168	1.4080		
Total	13185	18574.3886			

the organizational means and major organizational commitments . . . are directed, and which, in cases of conflict with goals which are stated but command few resources, have clear priority."[51]

Each discipline conceives a different goal or objective in its examination of profit-oriented organizations. The discipline of economics, for example, in its neoclassical approach views profit maximization as the single determinant of be-

havior. As seen in a previous chapter, organizational and management theories
have provided various behavioral theories of the firm. In management accounting, as in corporate finance, neither the economic model nor the behavioral
model appears entirely suitable. In fact, both models have influenced three held
views of business behavior applicable to management accounting: the shareholder wealth maximization model, the managerial welfare maximization model,
and the social welfare maximization model.[52] Each of these models constitutes
an acceptable objective of profit-oriented organizations in the field of management accounting. Because the scope and practice of management accounting is
heavily influenced by these assumptions, each of them is examined next.

2.7.2 The Shareholder Wealth Maximization Model

In most textbooks in the field of corporate finance and specifically in management accounting, authors operate on the assumption that management's primary goal is to maximize the wealth of its stockholders. This view is referred to
as the shareholder wealth maximization (SWM) model. According to this model,
the firm accepts all projects yielding more than the cost of capital, and in equity
financing, it prefers retaining earnings to issuing new stocks. It also assumes that
earnings are objectively determined to show the true financial position of the
firm to its owners and other users. In fact, the SWM model translates into maximizing the price of the common stock. Management is assumed to use decision
rules and techniques that are in the best interests of the stockholders. In a management accounting context, SWM implies an acceptance by management of
budgeting and control standards, a rejection of slack budgeting, any subopti-
mizing behavior, and an adoption of management accounting techniques that
are in the best interests of the owners of the firm. If management behaves otherwise, its right to manage may be either questioned or revoked, given that
stockholders own the firm and elect the management team. E. Solomon made a
similar suggestion as follows:

> But what if management has other motives, such as maximizing sales or
> size, growth or market share, or their own survival, or peace of mind?
> These operating goals do not necessarily conflict with the operating goal
> of wealth maximization. Indeed, a good case could be made for the thesis
> that wealth maximization also maximizes the achievement of these other
> objectives. But the point of issue is what if there is a conflict? What, for
> example, if management's quest for its own peace of mind or for some
> other goal consistently leads it to reject operating decisions that should be
> accepted by the wealth-maximizing criterion? The traditional answer is
> that such a management will be replaced sooner or later, and this is the
> only answer possible. Legally, management governs only as the appointed
> representatives of the owners. It may reject over-all goals so long as it
> substitutes goals which are designed to promote that of society as a

whole. But if it rejects owner-oriented goals and socially-oriented goals in favor of goals that are solely management-oriented and which lead to substantially different courses of action, its right to govern is open to question.[53]

2.7.3 The Managerial Welfare Maximization Model

Another school of thought maintains that a different objective function other than shareholder wealth maximization exists for the firm—namely, that managers run firms for their own benefits. It is maintained that because the stock of most large firms is widely held, the managers of such firms have a great deal of freedom. This being the case, they may be tempted for personal benefits to pursue an objective other than shareholder welfare maximization. This school of thought is generally referred to as the managerial welfare maximization (MWM) model. So rather than maximizing profits, the managers may maximize sales or assets,[54] the rate of growth,[55] or managerial utility.[56] As a consequence, managers may engage in suboptimization schemes as long as they contribute to their own welfare. For example, an entrenched management may avoid risky ventures even though the returns to stockholders would be high enough to justify the endeavor. In a management accounting context, MWM implies a lesser acceptance by management of budgeting and control standards, a recourse to slack budgeting and any suboptimization behavior, a manipulation or avoidance within legality of full disclosure in order to present the firm's operation favorably (i.e., income smoothing), and, finally, adoption of management accounting techniques that are in the best interest of managers. In a recent survey, B. Branch concludes as follows: "The evidence to date may be summarized as follows. Many managers have considerable discretion to substitute their own interests for that of the stockholders. Stockholder and manager interests can conflict or be independent in significant respects. The extent to which firms are managed in stockholder interests vary considerably. Most of the empirical work suggests that firms managed in stockholders' interests tend in some sense to out-perform management-oriented firms."[57]

That managers may elect to substitute their own different interests raises the question of how goals within MWM are "determined" or "set" in decisions to commit the organization to a particular course of action. Three distinct models have been identified to represent the goal-setting processes: The bargaining model, the problem-solving model, and the coalition model.[58] Because they present good conceptualizations of the goal determination process under MWM, they are briefly presented next.[59]

The Bargaining Model. The bargaining model depicts goal determination as the result of an open-minded negotiation process among all interested parties leading to a series of trade-offs and compromises. It is based on three important assumptions:

1. There is an active group of participants (internal or external) who impose demands on the organization.
2. These demands are conflicting; they cannot be accommodated simultaneously.
3. The individuals or groups are interdependent.[60]

The Problem-Solving Model. The problem-solving model describes goal determination as the result of successive decisions made by high-level administrators. It is based on three important assumptions:

1. Policy commitments are made within a set of constraints or requirements that are known to decision makers.
2. These constraints can be ranked and a preferred set accommodated.
3. The goals of different individuals or groups can be simultaneously satisfied.[61]

The Dominant Coalition Model. Given the existence of controlling interests in the firm, the dominant coalition model describes goal determination as the result of decisions made by those who control the ends to which policies and resources are committed. It is based on two assumptions:

1. There are many persons or groups who hold goals for an organization. These goals are frequently in conflict and cannot all be accommodated.
2. One individual or group does not have sufficient power alone to act unilaterally. Power is dispersed. Collective behavior is required to secure support for goals.[62]

2.7.4 The Social Welfare Maximization Model

The climate in which businesses operate is changing with pressures on organizations to be more sensitive to the impact of behavior on society. In adopting a more socially responsible attitude and responding to the pressures of new dimensions—social, human, and environmental—organizations may have to alter their main objective, whether SWM or MWM, to include as an additional constraint the welfare of society at large. This view may be referred to as the social welfare maximization (SOWM) model. Under SOWM, the firm undertakes all projects that, in addition to the usual profitability objective, minimize the social costs and maximize social benefits created by the productive operations of the firm. Thus, under SOWM the firm is not only liable to the shareholders and managers, but also to the society at large. Given the different interest groups in the society at large, the organization may have to develop different corporate purposes. For example, it was reported that one group has defined eight corporate purposes: "profit, sensitivity to natural and human environment, growth, responsiveness to consumer needs, equitable distributions of benefits, dynamic business structure, fair treatment of employees, and legal and ethical behavior."[63]

In a management accounting context, SOWM implies the development of a social reporting system oriented toward the measurement of social performance, including not only social costs but also social benefits. It suggests the development of a new concept of organization performance that will be more indicative of the firm's social responsibility than is provided by conventional accounting. For example, the AAA Committee on Measurement of Social Cost suggested a total organization performance, which is a function of "five outputs":

1. Net income, which benefits stockholders and provides resources for further business growth

2. Human resource contribution, which assists the individual in the organization to develop new knowledge or skills

3. Public contribution, which helps the organization's community to function and provides services for its constituency

4. Environmental contribution (closely allied with public contribution), which affects "quality of life" for society

5. Product or service contribution, which affects customer well-being and satisfaction[64]

Although a theory of social accounting is still emerging in the new public interest accounting paradigm, the proposed objectives and concepts for social accounting offer an interesting beginning.

However, regardless of the objective function adopted by managers, social reporting and particularly social reports are needed by management for relevant decision making and to comply with both social pressures and legal requirements.

2.7.5 Relationships between Organizational Slack and Profitability

Organizational slack is more likely in an organizational environment conducive to the managerial welfare maximization model. This is the context in which the model of the relationship between organizational slack and profitability will be developed.

For every firm there is a potential income that is determined and influenced by firm and industry factors, such as

$$PI = f(FF, IF)$$

where

PI = Potential income
FF = Firm factors
IF = Industry factors.

Each firm is, however, required to report its income that can be used to meet internal and external expectations. The reported income is different from the potential income because of all the adjustments made to meet these internal and external adjustments, such as

$$RI = f(PI, I\&EA)$$

where

RI   = Reported income
PI   = Potential income
I&EA = Internal and external adjustments.

The internal and external adjustments are of two kinds: (1) either an altering of the actual resources distributions and/or (2) using discretionary accruals to manage earnings. The second type of adjustment is known as earnings management. It is accomplished through changes in accounting procedures, through specific transactions such as debt defeasance or write-downs, and through discretion over accruals.[65] The focus on this chapter is not on the adjustments through earnings management but on the adjustments through organizational slack. Basically it is hypothesized that reported income is affected by organizational slack, such as

$$RI = (PI, OS)$$

where

RI = Reported income
PI = Potential income
OS = Organizational slack.

Basically organizational slack is used to absorb a substantial share of the variability of potential income in a systematic fashion. Organizational slack is used to stabilize potential income in two ways: "(1) by absorbing excess resources, it retards upward adjustment of aspirations during relatively good times; (2) by providing a pool of emergency resources, it permits aspirations to be maintained (and achieved) during relatively bad times."[66]

Basically reported level of income and reported variance of income are negatively related to organizational slack measures: administrative slack, available liquidity, and recoverable liquidity, such as

$$RI_i = a_0 - a_1 LAS_i - a_2 LAL_i - a_3 LRL_i + M_i$$

and

$$VRI_i = a_0' - a_1' VAS_i - a_2' VAL_i - a_3' VRL_i + M_i'$$

where

RI_i	=	Reportable income over sales
LAS_i	=	Level of administrative slack
LAL_i	=	Level of available liquidity
LRL_i	=	Level of recoverable liquidity
VRI_i	=	Variance of reportable income over sales
VAS_i	=	Variance of administrative slack
VAL_i	=	Variance of available liquidity
VRL_i	=	Variance of recoverable liquidity.

2.7.6 U.S. Evidence on Organizational Slack and Profitability

The tested hypotheses is that (1) the level of reportable income is negatively related to the levels of administrative slack, available liquidity, and recoverable liquidity and (2) the variance of reportable income is negatively related to the variance of administrative slack, available liquidity, and recoverable liquidity.

Exhibits 2.18 and 2.19 show, respectively, the regression results of the effects of slack on profits and the effects of the variance of slack on variance of profit.

The regression coefficients of these measures of organizational slack are significant with the correct sign. Both results show that (1) the level of reported income is negatively related to the levels of administrative slack, available liquidity and recoverable liquidity and (2) the variance of profit is negatively related to the variances of administrative slack, available liquidity, and recoverable liquidity.

Basically, as hypothesized, organizational slack is used to affect the level of profitability and/or absorb a substantial share of the variability of potential income.

Organizational slack appears as a tool created in the organization to provide stability to the organization. *In good times, it is used to absorb excess resources and retards upward adjustment of aspirations. In bad times, it is used to provide a pool of emergency resources and to permit aspirations to be maintained and achieved.*

2.8 CONCLUSIONS

This chapter examined two specific research questions: (1) Do the differences among U.S. firms in terms of type of membership in stock exchanges, fiscal year ending, and membership in economic sector lead to differences in organizational slack? and (2) Are the level and variance in the profitability of U.S. firms related to the level and variance in organizational slack? The following results were obtained:

Exhibit 2.18
Analysis of Variance: Effects of Levels of Slack on Profits

Variable	Intercept	Administrative Slack	Available Liquidity	Recoverable Liquidity	F Value	R2
Coefficients	0.056701	-0.11206	-0.0208	-0.0047	199.187*	5.09%
T statistic	(10.970)*	(-23.828)*	(-3.777)*	(-0.894)		

* Significant at α = 0.01

Exhibit 2.19
Analysis of Variance: Effects of Variance of Slack on Variance of Profit

Variable	Intercept	Variance Administrative Slack	Variance Available Liquidity	Variance Recoverable Liquidity	F Value	R2
Coefficients	0.073595	0.12319	0.11171	0.51811	177.304*	22.75%
T statistic	(1.563)	(6.082)*	(8.751)*	(14.984)*		

* Significant at α = 0.01

1. The results on all types of slack show that slack is the highest for firms listed on the American Stock Exchange.

2. The results on administrative slack show that this measure of slack is highest for "non-December" firms.

3. The results on both available and recoverable liquidity show that these two measures of organizational slack are the highest for "December" firms.

4. Administrative slack, available liquidity and recoverable liquidity are higher for firms in the periphery sector than in the core sector.

5. In good times, organizational slack is used to absorb excess resources and retards upward adjustment of aspirations. In bad times, it is used to provide a pool of emergency resources, and to permit aspirations to be maintained and achieved.

NOTES

1. B. F. King, "Market and Industry Factors in Stock Market Behavior," *Journal of Business* 39 (1966): 139–190.

2. T. J. Frecka, "The Effects of Complex Capital Structure on the Market Value of Firms," *Financial Review* (September, 1982): 86–111.

3. D. B. Smith and S. Pourcian, "A Comparison of Financial Characteristics of December and non-December Year-End Companies," *Journal of Accounting and Economics* 10 (1988): 335–344.

4. R. K. Atiase, "Predisclosure Information, Firm Capitalization, and Security Price Behavior Around Earnings Announcements," *Journal of Accounting Research* 32 (1985): 21–26.

5. O. E. Williamson, "A Model of Rational Managerial Behavior," in Richard M. Cyert and James G. March, *A Behavioral Theory of the Firm* (Englewood Cliffs, N.J.: Prentice-Hall, 1963).

6. L. J. Bourgeois and J. V. Singh, "Organizational Slack and Political Behavior Within Top Management Teams," *Academy of Managerial Proceedings* 24 (1983): 43–47.

7. J. V. Singh, "Performance Slack and Risk Taking in Strategic Decisions: Test of A Structural Equation Model," Ph.D. Thesis, Stanford Graduate School of Business, 1983.

8. Ibid.

9. Bourgeois and Singh, "Organizational Slack and Political Behavior Within Top Management Teams."

10. Ibid.

11. G. C. Cain, "The Challange of Segmented Labor Market Theories to Orthodox Theory: A Survey," *Journal of Economic Literature* 14 (1976): 1215–1257.

12. R. Hodson, and R. L. Kaufman, "Economic Dualism: A Critical Review," *American Sociological Review* (December 1982): 727–739.

13. E. M. Beck, P. N. Horan, and C. M. Tolbert II, "Stratification in a Dual Economy: A Sectoral Model of Earnings Determination," *American Sociological Review* 43 (1978): 704–720.

14. B. Harrison, "The Theory of the Dual Economy," in B. Silverman and M. Yanovitch, eds., *The Worker in Post Industrial Capitalism* (New York: Free Press, 1974), pp. 269–282.

15. S. Spilerman, "Careers Labor Market Structure and Socioeconomic Achievement," *American Journal of Sociology* 93 (1977): 551–593.

16. M. Piore, "The Dual Labor Market: Theory and Implications," in *Problems in Political Economy: An Urban Perspective* (Lexington, Mass.: Heath, 1977), p. 93.

17. R. T. Averitt, *The Dual Economy: The Dynamics of American Industry Structure* (New York: Horton, 1968).

18. B. Bluestone, W. M. Murphy, and M. Stevenson, *Low Wages and the Working Poor* (Ann Arbor: Institute of Labor and Industrial Relations, University of Michigan, 1973).

19. P. A. Baran, and P. M. Sweezy, *Monopoly Capital* (New York: Monthly Review Press, 1966).

20. Averitt, *The Dual Economy: The Dynamics of American Industry Structure*, p. 7.

21. Bluestone, Murphy, and Stevenson, *Low Wages and the Working Poor*, pp. 88–89.

22. J. O'Connor, *The Fiscal Crisis of the State* (New York: St. Martin's Press, 1973).

23. Hodson and Kaufman, "Economic Dualism: A Critical Review," p. 729.

24. Averitt, *The Dual Economy: The Dynamics of American Industry Structure*.

25. B. Bluestone, "The Tripartite Economy: Labor Markets and the Working Poor," *Poverty and the Human Resource Abstracts* 5 (1970): 15–35.

26. O'Connor, *The Fiscal Crisis of the State*.

27. J. K. Galbraith, *Economics and the Political Purpose* (Boston: Houghton Mifflin, 1973).

28. G. Oster, "A Factor Analytic Test of the Theory of the Dual Economy," *Review of Economics and Statistics* 61 (1979): 33–39.

29. R. Bibbs and W. Form, "The Effects of Industrial, Occupational and Sex Stratification on Wages in Blue-Collar Markets," *Social Forces* 55 (1977): 974–996.

30. Beck, Horan, and Tolbert II, "Stratification in a Dual Economy: A Sectoral Model of Earnings Determination."

31. Averitt, *The Dual Economy: The Dynamics of American Industry Structure*.

32. Bluestone, Murphy, and Stevenson, *Low Wages and the Working Poor*.

33. R. Hodson, "Labor in the Monopoly, Competitive and State Sectors of Production," *Politics and Society* 8 (1978): 429–480.

34. Oster, "A Factor Analytic Test of the Theory of the Dual Economy."

35. C. Tolbert, P. Horan, and E. M. Beck, "The Structure of Economic Segmentation: A Dual Economy Approach," *American Journal of Sociology* 85 (1980): 1095–1116.

36. Hodson, "Labor in the Monopoly, Competitive and State Sectors of Production."

37. Oster, "A Factor Analytic Test of the Theory of the Dual Economy."

38. Tolbert, Horan, and Beck, "The Structure of Economic Segmentation: A Dual Economy Approach."

39. Beck, Horan, and Tolbert II, "Stratification in a Dual Economy: A Sectoral Model of Earnings Determination."

40. Bibbs and Form, "The Effects of Industrial, Occupational, and Sex Stratification on Wages in Blue-Collar Markets."

41. This classification method is subject to various qualifications. The characteristics of industries and/or firms may not be uniquely attributable to a binomial distribution. For

example, it is assumed that all industry members are collectively classified as either core or periphery, and firms are classified into a single industry by its primary line of business. However, industries may not be homogeneous and firms can have several lines of business. Furthermore, industry relationships and, therefore, dual classifications may change over time because of changes in technology, foreign competition, and the like.

42. Philip Karpik and Ahmed Riahi-Belkaoui, "A Comparison of Financial Characteristics of Companies in the Core and Periphery Economies," *Advances in Quantitative Analysis in Finance and Accounting* (forthcoming).

43. The probability of a firm in the core sector is P_{cs}, whereas the probability that it will be in the periphery sector is $1 - P_{cs}$. The predicted value of the dependent variable is therefore the maximum likelihood estimate of the natural logarithm of the odds that the firm in question is in the core sector.

44. The logistic model was also run with sales inventory turnover (SIT) and/or sales receivable turnover (SRT) variables, the overall results are not materially different. Although these terms were statistically significant at a 0.05 level, including either turnover measure considerably reduced the subsample of periphery firms, thereby reducing the overall power of the model.

45. Several factors may explain the lack of significance for the size term. Total assets are highly correlated with the current ratio and capital intensity measure. Another likely explanation is that firms issuing publicly traded equity and that are included in the Compustat files tend to be larger and more successful, thus there is a bias against periphery firms that are likely to be smaller and less successful.

46. Amitai Etzioni, *Modern Organizations* (Englewood Cliffs, N.J.: Prentice-Hall, 1964), p. 3.

47. Richard H. Hall, *Organizations: Structure and Process* (Englewood Cliffs, N.J.: Prentice-Hall, 1972), p. 9.

48. V. Buck, "The Organization as a System of Constraints," in J. D. Thompson, ed., *Approaches to Organization Design* (Pittsburgh: The University of Pittsburgh Press, 1966), p. 109.

49. J. D. Thompson, *Organizations in Action* (New York: McGraw-Hill, 1967), p. 128.

50. C. Perrow, "The Analysis of Goals in Complex Organizations," *American Sociological Review* 26 (1961): 854–866.

51. Etzioni, *Modern Organizations*, p. 7.

52. Chapman M. Findlay and G. A. Whitmore, "Beyond Shareholder Wealth Maximization," *Financial Management* (Winter 1974): 25–35.

53. E. Solomon, *The Theory of Financial Management* (New York: Columbia University Press, 1963), p. 24.

54. W. Baumol, *Business Behavior, Value and Growth* (New York: Macmillan, 1964).

55. R. Marris, *The Economic Theory of Managerial Capitalism* (London: Macmillan, 1964).

56. A. Papandreou, "Some Basic Issues in the Theory of the Firm," in B. Haley, ed., *A Survey of Contemporary Economics* (Homewood, Ill.: Richard D. Irwin, 1952); O. Williamson, *The Economics of Discretionary Behavior: Managerial Objectives in the Theory of the Firm* (Englewood Cliffs, N.J.: Prentice-Hall, 1964).

57. B. Branch, "Corporate Objectives and Market Performance," *Financial Management* (Summer 1973): 24–29.

58. Francine S. Hall, "Organizational Goals: The Status of Theory and Research," in J. Leslie Livingstone, ed., *Managerial Accounting: The Behavioral Foundations* (Columbus, Ohio: Grid, 1975), pp. 1–29.

59. For an excellent presentation of these models, the reader is advised to examine the article by Hall in ibid.

60. Ibid., p. 17.

61. Ibid., p. 20.

62. Ibid., p. 23.

63. American Accounting Association, Committee on Measurement of Social Costs, "Report of the Committee on the Measurement of Social Costs," *The Accounting Review* 69 (supplement, 1974): 100–136.

64. Ibid., pp. 101–102.

65. Maureen McNichols and G. Peter Wilson, "Evidence of Earnings Management from the Provision for Bad Debts," *Journal of Accounting Research* 26 (supplement 1988): 1–31.

66. Richard M. Cyert and James G. March, *A Behavioral Theory of the Firm* (Englewood Cliffs, N.J.: Prentice-Hall, 1963), p. 38.

SELECTED BIBLIOGRAPHY

Averitt, R. T. *The Dual Economy*. New York: W.W. Norton, 1968.

Baran, P. A., and P. M. Sweezy. *Monopoly Capital: An Essay on the American Economic and Social Order*. New York: Monthly Review Press, 1965.

Baron, J. N., and W. T. Bielly. "Bringing the Firms Back In: Stratification, Segmentation, and the Organization of Work." *American Sociological Review* 45 (1990): 11–52.

Baron, H. M., and B. Hymer. "The Negro Worker in the Chicago Labor Market." In J. Jacobson, ed., *The Negro and the American Labor Movement*. New York: Doubleday, 1968.

Beck, E. M., P. M. Horan, and C. M. Tolbert. "Stratification in the Dual Economy: A Sectorial Model of Earnings Determination." *American Sociological Review* 43 (1978): 704–720.

Berger, S., and M. J. Piore. *Dualism and Discontinuity in Industrial Societies*. Cambridge, England: Cambridge University Press, 1980.

Bibb R., and W. Form. "The Effects of Industrial, Occupational, and Sex Stratification on Wages in Blue Collar Markets." *Social Forces* 55 (1977): 974–996.

Bluestone, B. "The Tripatriate Economy: Labor Markets and the Working Poor." *Poverty and Human Resources* 5 (1970): 15–35.

Bluestone, B., W. M. Murphy, and M. Stevenson. *Low Wages and the Working Poor*. Ann Arbor: Institute of Labor and Industrial Relations, University of Michigan, 1973.

Boeke, J. H. *Economies and Economic Policy of Dual Societies*. Harlem: Tjeenk Willink, 1983.

Bourgeois, L. J., and J. V. Singh. "Organizational Slack and Political Behavior Within Top Management Teams." *Academy of Management Proceedings* (1983): 43–47.

Bronfenbrenmer, M. "Radical Economies in America: A 1970 Survey." *Journal of Economic Literature* (September 1970): 97–120.

Doeringer, P., and M. Piore. *Internal Labor Markets and Manpower Analysis*. Lexington, Mass. D. C. Heath, 1971.

Edwards, R. C. "The Social Relations of Production in the Firm and Labor Market Structure." In R. C. Edwards, M. Reich, and D. M. Gordon, eds., *Labor Market Segmentation*. Lexington, Mass.: D. C. Heath, 1975.

————. *Contested Terrain*. New York: Basic Books, 1979.

Edwards, R. C., M. Reich, and D. M. Gordon, eds. *Labor Market Segmentation*. Lexington, Mass. D.C. Heath, 1975.

Furnivall, J. S. *Netherlands and India: A Study of Plural Economy*. New York: Macmillan, 1944.

————. *Colonial Policy and Practice*. Cambridge, England: Cambridge University Press, 1948.

Galbraith, J. K. *Economies and the Public Purpose*. Boston: Houghton Mifflin, 1973.

Gordon, D. M. *Theories of Poverty and Underemployment*. Lexington, Mass. D.C. Heath, 1979.

Harrison, B. *Education, Training, and the Urban Ghetto*. Baltimore: Johns Hopkins University Press, 1972.

Hodson, R. "Labor in the Monopoly, Competitive, and State Sectors of Production." *Politics and Society* 8 (1978): 95–105.

Hodson, R., and R. L. Kaufman. "Economic Dualism: A Critical Review." *American Sociological Review* (December 1982): 727–739.

Kalleberg, A. L., R. Wallace, and R. P. Althauser. "Economic Segmentation, Worker Power, and Income Inequality." *American Journal of Sociology* 87 (1981): 45–62.

Karpik, Philip, and Ahmed Riahi-Belkaoui. "A Comparison of the Financial Characteristics of Companies in the Core and Periphery Economies." *Advances in Quantitative Analysis in Finance and Accounting* (forthcoming).

O'Connor, J. *The Fiscal Crisis of the State*. New York: St. Martin's Press, 1973.

Osterman, P. "An Empirical Study of Labor Market Segmentation." *Industrial and Labor Relations Review* 28 (1975): 67–73.

Piore, M. J. "The Dual Labor Market: Theory and Implications." In S. H. Beer and R. E. Beringer, eds., *The State and the Poor*. New York: Winthrop, 1970.

Piore, M. J. "Jobs and Training." In S. H. Beer and R. E. Barringer, eds., *The State and the Poor*. Boston: Winthrop, 1970.

Reich, M., D. M. Gordon, and R. C. Edwards. "A Theory of Labor Market Segmentation." *American Economic Review* 63 (1973): 78–90.

Riahi-Belkaoui, Ahmed. *The New Foundations of Management Accounting*. Westport, Conn.: Quorum, 1992.

Singh, J. V. *Performance Slack and Risk Taking in Strategic Decisions: Test of a Structural Equation Model*. Ph.D. Thesis, Stanford Graduate School of Business, 1983.

Smith, D. B., and S. Pourcian. "A Comparison of Financial Characteristics of December and Non-December Year-End Companies." *Journal of Accounting and Economics* 10 (1988): 335–344.

Stolzenberg, R. M. "Bringing the Boss Back In: Employer Size, Employee Schooling, and Socioeconomic Achievement." *American Sociological Review* 43 (1978): 42–53.

Thurow, L. C. *Generating Inequality*. New York: Basic Books, 1975.

Tolbert, C. M., II, P. M. Horan, and E. M. Beck. "The Structure of Economic Segmentation: A Dual Economy Approach." *American Journal of Sociology* 85 (1980): 1095–1116.

Victoisz, T., and B. Harrison. *The Economic Development of Harlem.* New York: Praeger, 1970.

Wachtel, H. M. "The Impact of Labor Market Conditions on Hard-Core Unemployment." *Poverty and Human Resources* (July-August, 1970): 5–13.

Williamson, O. E. "A Model of Rational Managerial Behavior." In Richard M. Cyert and James G. March, eds., *A Behavioral Theory of the Firm.* Englewood Cliffs, N.J.: Prentice-Hall, 1963.

3

Organizational Slack and Multidivisional Structure: The Contingency of Diversification Strategy

3.1 INTRODUCTION

The multidivisional (M-form) structure has evolved as a more popular solution to the problems of managing growth and diversity within a centralized (U-form) structure. It is generally presented as providing information-processing advantages, as well as better performance in large multiproduct firms.[1] Although implied by Williamson,[2] the impact of the M-form implementation on organizational slack remains unexplored. This chapter examines the proposition that the impact of the implementation of such structure on organizational slack should vary with the diversification strategy adopted. More specifically, given the trade-off between control system emphases in various diversification strategies, certain controls are better at reducing certain types of slack in certain strategies. In what follows, the M-form hypothesis, diversification strategies, and organizational slack are examined before a presentation of the central proposition and empirical results.

3.2 THE MULTIDIVISIONAL FORM HYPOTHESIS

In a major historical study of American enterprise, A. G. Chandler[3] noted that in the early 1920s the multidivisional structure was adopted as a response to the increasingly complex administrative problems encountered within a centralized functional (U-form) structure as firm size and diversity increased. Building on Chandler's analysis, Williamson suggested that because of two problems encountered by expanding multiproduct firms—cumulative control loss and confounding of strategic and operating decision making—there is the risk of failure to achieve least-cost profit maximization behavior.[4] Basically, he maintained that as size increases, people reach their limits of control as a result of bounded rationality and start resorting to opportunism, thereby threatening efficiency and profitability. The M-form is presented as a unique structural framework that overcomes these difficulties and favors goal pursuits and least-cost behavior more nearly associated with the neoclassical profit-maximizing hypotheses.

In fact, Neil Fligstein (1985) proposed five theories that can be used to explain the genesis of the multidivisional form, namely,

1. *Strategy-structure*,[5] whereby firms' diversification strategy called for a multidivisional structure;

2. *Transaction-cost analysis* as enunciated by Williamson,[6] whereby firms may be more inclined to choose the multidivisional form because the continuous expansion of the unitary of functional form creates "cumulative control loss" effects, which have internal efficiency consequences;

3. *Population-ecology theory*, as enunciated by M. Hannan and J. Freeman,[7,8] whereby, given the link between organizational niche, age, and inertia and the possibility of organizational change, one would expect that younger and smaller firms would be more likely to adopt the multidivisional form;

4. *Control theory based on power*, as enunciated by J. Pfeffer[9,10] and Pfeffer and G. Salancik,[11] whereby the multidivisional form would be favored by the new power holders, sales and marketing and finance personnel, because the M-form allows for growth through product related and unrelated strategies; and

5. *Organizational homogeneity theory* as enunciated by P. DiMaggio and W. Powell,[12] whereby large organizations start mimicking one another structurally by adopting the multidivisional form as a result of three kinds of environmental pressures: (a) the cultural expectations of competitors, suppliers and the state; (b) the environmental uncertainty; and (c) a particular world view of appropriate behavior created by the professionalization of managers.

Based on the transaction cost analysis, researchers investigated a hypothesis of links between the M-form structure and better performance. Results to date provided either a support of the proposition that the M-form implementation affects performance in large corporations regardless of other contingencies,[13,14,15,16,17,18,19,20] or mixed results.[21,22,23] These studies did not differentiate among the firms on the basis of their diversification strategy. One exception by R. E. Hoskisson[24] provided evidence in support of a contingency view of the relationship between performance and implementation of the M-form structure. These studies examine considerations of return and risk but not slack.

3.3 ORGANIZATIONAL SLACK

3.3.1 Organizational Slack Concepts

Because the definition of slack is often intertwined with a description of the functions that slack serves, Bourgeois[25] discussed these functions as a means of making palpable the ways of measuring slack. From a review of the administrative theory literature, he identified organizational slack as an independent variable that either "causes or serves four primary functions" (1) as an instrument for organizational actors to remain in the system, a form of inducement;[26,27,28] (2) as a resource for conflict resolution;[29] (3) as a technical buffer from the variances and discontinuities created by environmental uncertainty;[30,31] and (4) as a facilitator of certain types of strategic or creative behavior,[32] providing opportunities for a satisfying behavior,[33] and promoting political behavior.[34]

3.3.2 Derived Measures of Organizational Slack

One of the problems of empirically investigating the presence of organizational slack relates to the difficulties of securing adequate measurement for the phenomenon. Various ad hoc measures based on questionnaires, interviews or archival measures were proposed.[35] In addition to these methods, Bourgeois identified eight variables that appear in public data, whether created by managerial actions or made available by the environment, and may explain a change in slack. The model suggested is as follows:

$$Slack = f(RE, DP, G{\circ}A, WC/Sales, D/E, CR, I/P, P/E)$$

where

RE	=	Retained earnings
DP	=	Dividend payout
G∘A	=	General and administrative expenses
WC/S	=	Working capital as a percentage of sales
D/E	=	Debt as a percentage of equity
CR	=	Credit rating
I/P	=	Short term loan interest compared to prime rate
P/E	=	Price/earnings ratio.

RE, G∘A, WC/S, and CR are assumed to have a positive effect on changes in slack, whereas DP, D/E, and I/P are assumed to have a negative effect on changes in slack. For example, Rosner[36] used profit and excess capacity as slack measures. Bourgeois and Singh[37] refined these measures by suggesting that slack can be differentiated on an "ease of recovery dimension." A distinction is made between *absorbed slack*, slack that has been absorbed as cost in the organization, and *unabsorbed slack*, referring to excess liquidity not yet earmarked for particular uses.[38]

Absorbed slack was measured by the level of general and administrative expenses divided by the cost of goods sold. This concept of absorbed slack, also referred to as *administrative slack*, captures slack absorbed as costs. It follows from Williamson's[39] notion of slack as extra staff that can be reduced in difficult times.

Unabsorbed slack was measured by the sum of cash and marketable securities minus current liabilities divided by sales. It follows the notion of slack as readily accessible resources not absorbed by costs, thus giving the amount of liquid resources uncommitted to liabilities in the near future.

3.4 DIVERSIFICATION STRATEGY AND CONTROL

J. R. Galbraith and D. A. Nathanson[40] traced the growth of firms in three major categories of corporate diversification strategy: vertical integration, related business diversification, and unrelated business diversification.

Vertical integration offers the firm economies due to control of its supply/output markets. The firm's value added margin for a chain of processing is increased due to increased control over raw materials and/or outlets.[41,42,43] Furthermore, market transaction costs, such as opportunistic actions by traders or the drafting and monitoring of contingent claims contracts to ensure harmonious trading relationships, can either be eliminated or reduced.[44]

Firms pursuing a strategy of related diversification can realize synergistic economies of scope through the joint use of inputs.[45,46] Exploitation of this energy is achieved through both tangible and intangible interrelationships.[47] Tangible interrelationships are created by such devices as joint procurement of raw materials, joint development of shared technologies or production processes, joint sales forces, and joint physical distribution systems. Intangible interrelationships arise from the sharing of know-how and capabilities.

An unrelated diversification strategy is assumed to yield financial economies. The risk of pooling of imperfectly correlated income streams created by unrelated diversification is, in principle, assumed to produce an asset with superior risk/return relationship.[48]

The differences in economic characteristics among the three types of strategies create situations that may call for different types of control. It is suggested that control arrangements within a basic M-form framework must be consistent with a firm's corporate diversification strategy if the firm is to realize the economic benefits associated with that strategy. Similarly, based on a review of a large body of research on strategy implementation, B. Baysinger and Hoskisson[49] conclude that firms pursuing a dominant or vertical strategy place a higher emphasis on strategic control than related and unrelated diversification, in that order, and a lower emphasis on financial controls than related and unrelated diversifiers, in that order.

3.5 THEORY AND HYPOTHESES

The M-form hypothesis predicts that under the U-form structure a fair degree of managerial slack would develop within each department, causing the creation of discretionary investment projects to justify the extra staff. The implementation of the M-form structure is expected to reduce this managerial slack and channel the operation of the firm toward goal pursuit and least-cost behavior more nearly associated with the neoclassical profit maximization hypothesis.[50]

The reduction of slack following the implementation of the M-form differs however, depending whether slack refer to absorbed or unabsorbed slack and on the diversification strategy adopted as follows:

A. If the diversification strategy adopted is a vertical integration or related diversification, a higher emphasis is placed on strategic controls than on financial controls. It eliminates the need for extra staff and discretionary investment projects, and the formulation of investment opportunities occurs at the top of the organization, or at the level of strategic business units.[51] Absorbed slack or administrative slack should, therefore, be expected to decrease following the implementation of the M-form by firms using either vertical integration or related diversification. The reduction of unabsorbed slack may be more difficult given the moderate or low reliance on financial controls.

B. If the diversification strategy adopted is an unrelated diversification, a higher emphasis is placed on financial control than on strategic control. It reduces the level of unabsorbed slack because cash flows are not automatically returned to their sources but, instead, are exposed to internal competition, and investment projects are evaluated on strict objective criteria. The reduction of absorbed slack may be more difficult as the extra staff needed to manage the large number of business units according to detailed strategic criteria and secure high accountability for divisional profits.

This suggests the following two hypotheses:

H1: Implementation of the M-form structure in vertically integrated and in related diversified leads to a decrease in absorbed slack.

H2: Implementation of the M-form structure in unrelated diversified firms leads to a decrease in unabsorbed slack.

3.6 METHODS

3.6.1 Sample and Data Collection

Previous research has identified sixty-two firms that adopted the M-form during the period 1950–1978.[52,53] The sample used in this study consists of these firms. Each firm was diversified at the time of the restructuring and is classified by R. P. Rumelt's[54] method as having being in one of three diversification classes—unrelated (sixteen firms), related (twenty-two firms), or vertical (twenty-four firms). Exhibit 3.1 lists the firms, their classification, and the year in which the restructuring occurred.

A longitudinal design is used to capture the effects over time of the implementation of the M-form. Data for two measures of slack were collected for year –5 through year +5 (relative to the year of restructuring). In addition, three covariates (growth in gross national product [GNP], growth in total assets, and firm size) and two control variables (early/late adoption of the M-form and industry classification) are used.

3.6.2 Dependent Variable

Financial statement data for years –5 to +5 (relative to the year of restructuring) for each firm were collected from Compustat. Year 0, relative to the year of restructuring, was excluded from the analysis to avoid the potential confounding of slack measures with events during the transition. The data collected were absorbed slack, computed as general and administrative costs divided by cost of goods sold, and absorbed slack, computed as cash plus marketable securities minus current liabilities divided by sales.

3.6.3 Control Variables and Covariates

Two control factors, early/late adoption of the M-form and industry classification, and three covariates, firm size, growth in total assets, and growth in GNP, are included to control for possible intervening effects.

The control factor, early/late adopter, is motivated by the belief that late adopters learn from the experience of early adopters and are thus able to restructure faster and more efficiently.[55] Early/late adoption is measured by the year of restructuring relative to the sample median. Hence, firms adopting the M-form structure prior to 1967 are classified as early movers and those adopting in 1967 or later are classified as late movers. The control factor of industry is included to control for industry effects. Firm size, asset growth rate, and GNP growth rate are included as covariates. Their use is motivated by (1) the suggestion that firms may sacrifice profitability in periods of growth[56] and (2) the need to control for changes in organizational slack related to major external shifts in aggregate demands. Firm size is measured as the proportional change in total

Exhibit 3.1
Companies and Year of Change

Companies	Year of Change
Vertically integrated firms	
ALCOA	1968
B. F. Goodrich	1953
Burlington	1962
City Service	1966
Continental Can	1950
Crown Zellerback	1968
Getty Oil	1959
Goodyear	1976
Hormel	1966
International Paper	1973
Kaiser Aluminum	1958
Kennecott Copper	1966
Marathon Oil	1963
Mobil Oil	1960
Occidental Petroleum	1971
Phillips Petroleum	1975
Shell Oil	1961
Standard Oil (California)	1955
Standard Oil of Ohio	1962
Standard Oil (Indiana)	1961
St. Regis Paper	1969
Sun Oil	1971
Union Oil	1964
Uniroyal	1960
Related-diversified firms	
Allied Chemical	1972
Ashland Oil	1970
Bendix	1965
Borden	1968
Burroughs	1966
Celanese	1963
Coca Cola	1968
CPC	1967
Dow Chemical	1963
General Foods	1952
Heinz	1967
Honeywell	1962
IBM	1965
Ingersoll Rand	1964
Monsanto	1971

(continued)

Exhibit 3.1   (Continued)

Companies	Year of Change
Phillip Morris	1967
Procter & Gamble	1966
Quaker Oats	1971
Ralston Purina	1968
R. J. Reynolds	1970
J. P. Stevens	1971
White Motor	1969

Unrelated-diversified firms

AMF	1958
Borg Warner	1970
Brunswick	1969
Colt Industries	1970
Dart Industries	1962
DAYCO	1966
Esmark	1970
FMC	1961
Gulf & Western	1967
ITT	1968
Lear Siegler	1969
Ogden	1960
Textron	1969
U.S. Industries	1959
Raytheon	1966
SCM	1962

assets, and GNP growth is measured as the proportional change in GNP. Each of the covariates is measured for the same period as the dependent variable.

3.7 DATA ANALYSIS

To test the overall relationship among (1) organizational structure and organizational slack, (2) diversification strategy and organizational slack, and (3) the interactive effect of organizational structure and diversification strategy on organizational slack, an analysis of covariance is used. Early/late adoption and industry membership are control variables; firm size, asset growth rate, and GNP growth rate are covariates. Hypotheses are tested by an *F* test of the difference among variances.

Exhibit 3.2 and 3.3 present the results of the analysis of covariance for absorbed and unabsorbed slack for the sixty-two firms in the sample. The results of the overall analysis of the covariance in both exhibits are highly significant and suggest that organizational structure and organizational slack as well as diversification strategy and organizational slack are related. The significant interaction effect in both exhibits between strategic type and the implementation of the M-

Exhibit 3.2
Results of Overall Analysis of Variance for the Absorbed Slack

Sources	F	P
Diversification Strategy	760.32	0.0001*
M. Form Implementation (before/after)	432.25	0.0001*
M. Form * Diversification Interaction	851.26	0.0001*
Control Variable		
Early/late adopter	2.85	0.094**
Covariates		
Size	0.00	0.947
Total Asset Growth	0.16	0.685
Total Growth in GNP	1.08	0.295
Industry	684.19	0.001*

° Significant at $\alpha = 0.01$
°° Significant at $\alpha = 0.10$

Exhibit 3.3
Results of Overall Analysis of Variance for the Unabsorbed Slack

Sources	F	P
Diversification Strategy	5.76	0.0061*
M. Form Implementation (before/after)	7.06	0.0110**
M. Form * Diversification Interaction	2.33	0.0032*
Control Variable		
Early/late adopter	2.87	0.094**
Covariates		
Size	0.00	0.945
Total Asset Growth	0.17	0.683
Total Growth in GNP	1.09	0.299
Industry	2.29	0.0033*

° Significant at $\alpha = 0.01$
°° Significant at $\alpha = 0.10$

Exhibit 3.4

T Tests and Slack Measures Means and Standard Deviations by Strategy Types before and after M-Form Implementation

Measures	Before M-Form		After M-Form		
	Mean	Standard Deviation	Mean	Standard Deviation	t
A. Vertically Integrated Firms					
1. Absorbed Slack	0.16744	0.08610	0.14860	0.0674	0.8260
2. Unabsorbed Slack	-0.05838	0.007711	-0.10210	0.0689	2.1339*
B. Related-Diversified Firms					
1. Absorbed Slack	0.28156	0.18787	0.29270	0.20022	-0.1859
2. Unabsorbed Slack	-0.07611	0.1474	-0.1408	0.11942	1.5627**
C. Unrelated-Diversified Firms					
1. Absorbed Slack	2.6657	7.4874	0.20720	0.14642	1.2715**
2. Unabsorbed Slack	-0.16067	0.108448	-0.14640	0.06373	-0.4394

° Significant at $\alpha = 0.05$
°° Significant at $\alpha = 0.10$

form suggests that the M-form implementation had a differential impact on organizational slack depending on the diversification strategy adopted.

The impact of the M-form implementation on organizational slack is further investigated by performing mean comparisons of absorbed and unabsorbed slack before and after the M-form by strategic type. Exhibit 3.4 presents the results. It indicates that following the implementation of the M-form, vertically integrated and related diversified firms decreased their absorbed slack, whereas unrelated diversified firms decreased their unabsorbed slack, which is consistent with both H1 and H2.

3.8 DISCUSSION

The objective of this study was to show that the implementation of the M-form structure creates differences in organizational slack measures in firms that employ different diversification strategies. The slack measures used were absorbed for administrative slack and unabsorbed slack for available liquidity. The diversification strategies were related diversification, vertical integration, and unrelated diversification. The results show that the contingency view of the relationship between organizational slack and implementation of the M-form structure was supported for both absorbed and unabsorbed slack.

Hypothesis 1 was confirmed, suggesting that the implementation of a multidivisional structure leads to a reduction of absorbed slack or administrative slack in both vertically integrated and related diversified firms. This result follows from (1) the general thesis that the M-form reduces the organizational slack developed within each department under the U-form and (2) the particular thesis that vertically integrated and related diversified firms rely mostly on strategic controls that are most effective in monitoring expenditures on excess staff and discretionary expenses.

Hypothesis 2 was also confirmed, suggesting that the implementation of a multidivisional structure leads to reduction of unabsorbed slack of available liquidity in unrelated diversified firms. This result follows again from (1) the slack reduction thesis of the M-form hypothesis and (2) the particular thesis that unrelated diversified firms rely mostly on financial controls that are most effective in monitoring cash flows within the firm.

The results suggest that the M-form implementation increases the firm's capacity to manage absorbed slack in the cases of the vertically integrated and related diversified firms and unabsorbed slack in the case of unrelated diversified firms. It points to another additional benefit of the M-form, when coupled with the appropriate control system—strategic controls for the vertically integrated and related diversified firms and financial controls for the unrelated diversified firms. More benefits would result from an increase in the use of financial controls by the related diversified and vertically integrated firms, and in the use of strategic controls by the unrelated diversified firms. Obviously, more research is needed to verify these results using different measures of slack and/or using different companies from different periods and from different countries.

NOTES

1. D. J. Teece, "Internal Organization and Economic Performance: An Empirical Analysis of the Profitability of Principal Firms," *Journal of Industrial Economic* 30 (1981): 173–199.

2. O. E. Williamson, *Corporate Control and Business Behavior* (Englewood Cliffs, N.J.: Prentice-Hall, 1970).

3. A. G. Chandler, *Strategy and Structure: Chapters in the History of the American Industrial Enterprise* (Cambridge, Mass.: MIT Press, 1962).

4. W. Williamson, *Markets and Hierarchies: Analysis and Antitrust Implication* (New York: Free Press, 1975).

5. Chandler, *Strategy and Structure*.

6. Williamson, *Markets and Hierarchies: Analysis and Antitrust Implication*.

7. M. Hannan and J. Freeman, "The Population Ecology of Organizations," *American Journal of Sociology* 92 (1977): 929–964.

8. M. Hannan and J. Freeman, "Structural Inertia and Organizational Change," *American Sociological Review* 49 (1984): 149–164.

9. J. Pfeffer, *Power in Organizations* (Marshfield, Mass.: Pitman, 1981).

10. J. Pfeffer, *Organizations and Organizational Theory* (Marshfield, Mass.: Pitman, 1982).

11. J. Pfeffer and G. Salancik, *The External Control of Organizations: A Resource Dependency Perspective* (New York: Harper & Row, 1978).

12. P. DiMaggio and W. Powell, "Institutional Isomerphism," *American Sociological Review* 48 (1983): 147–160.

13. R. A. Armour and D. J. Teece, "Organizational Structure and Economic Performance: A Test of the Multidivisional Hypothesis," *Bell Journal of Economics* 9 (1978): 106–122.

14. M. A. Ezzamel and K. Hilton, "Divisionalization in British Industry: A Preliminary Study," *Accounting and Business Research* 10 (1980): 197–211.

15. B. C. Harris, *Organizations: The Effect of Large Corporations* (Ann Arbor, Mich.: UMI Research Press, 1983).

16. C.W.L. Hill, "Internal Organization and Enterprise Performance," *Managerial and Decision Economics* 6 (1985): 210–216.

17. R. E. Hoskisson and C. S. Galbraith, "The Effect of Quantum Versus Incremental M-form Reorganization on Performance: A Time-Series Exploration of Intervention Dynamics," *Journal of Management* 11 (1985): 55–70.

18. R. P. Rumelt, *Strategy, Structure and Economic Performance* (Cambridge, Mass: Harvard University Press, 1974).

19. P. Steer and J. Cable, "Internal Organization and Profit: An Empirical Analysis of Large U.K. Companies," *Journal of Industrial Economics* 30 (1981): 201–211.

20. J. D. Thompson, *Organizations in Action* (New York: McGraw-Hill, 1967).

21. R. E. Hoskisson, "Corporate Growth Strategy and Implementation of the Multidivisional Structure: The Effect of Risk, Return and Growth," *Southwest Academy of Management Proceedings* (1982): 33–37.

22. R. Buhner and P. Moller, "The Informational Content of Corporate Disclosure of Divisionalization Decisions," *Journal of Management Studies* 22 (1985): 309–321.

23. R. A. Bettis and A. Chen, "Organizational Structure and Financial Market Performance: A Preliminary Test," Working paper, Dallas: Southern Methodist University, 1986.

24. R. E. Hoskisson, "Multidivisional Structure and Performance: The Contingency of Diversification Strategy," *Academy of Management Journal* (December 1987): 625–644.

25. L. J. Bourgeois, "On the Measurement of Organizational Slack," *Academy of Management Review* 6 (1981): 29–39.

26. C. I. Barnard, *Functions of the Executive* (Cambridge, Mass.: Harvard University Press, 1938).

27. J. G. March and H. A. Simon, *Organizations* (New York: Wiley, 1958).

28. R. M. Cyert and J. G. March, *A Behavioral Theory of the Firm* (Englewood Cliffs, N.J.: Prentice-Hall, 1963).

29. L. R. Pondy, "Organizational Conflict: Concepts and Models," *Administrative Science Quarterly* 12 (1967): 296–320.

30. J. D. Thompson, *Organizations in Action* (New York: McGraw-Hill, 1967).

31. Jay Galbraith, *Designing Complex Organizations* (Reading, Mass.: Addison-Wesley, 1973).

32. D. C. Hambrick and C. C. Snow, "A Contextual Model of Strategic Decision Making in Organizations," in R. L. Taylor, J. J. O'Connell, R. A. Zawacki, and D. D. Warrick, eds., *Academy of Management Proceedings* (1977): 109–112.

33. H. A. Simon, *Administrative Behavior* (New York: Free Press, 1957).

34. W. G. Astley, "Sources of Power in Organizational Life," Unpublished doctoral dissertation, University of Washington, 1978.

35. Bourgeois, "On the Measurement of Organizational Slack," pp. 32, 35.

36. Martin M. Rosner, "Economic Determinants of Organizational Innovation," *Administrative Science Quarterly* 12 (1968): 614–625.

37. L. J. Bourgeois and J. V. Singh, "Organizational Slack and Political Behavior within Top Management," *Academy of Management Proceedings* (1983): 43–47.

38. L. J. Bourgeois and J. V. Singh, "Organizational Slack and Political Behavior within Top Management," *Academy of Management Proceedings* (1983): 43–47.

39. O. E. Williamson, "A Model of Rational Managerial Behavior," in R. M. Cyert and J. G. March, eds., *A Behavioral Theory of the Firm* (Englewood Cliffs, N.J.: Prentice-Hall, 1963).

40. J. R. Galbraith and D. A. Nathanson, "Role of Organizational Structure and Process in Strategic Implementation," in D. Schendel and C. Hofer, eds., *Strategic Management: A New View of Business Policy and Planning* (Boston: Little, Brown and Co., 1979), pp. 249–283.

41. J. Pfeffer and G. Salancik, *The External Control of Organizations: A Resource Dependency Perspective* (New York: Harper and Row, 1978).

42. F. M. Scherer, *Industrial Market Structure and Economic Performance* (Chicago: Rand McNally Co., 1984).

43. K. R. Harrigan, "Vertical Integration and Corporate Strategy," *Academy of Management Journal* 28 (1985): 397–425.

44. C. W. L. Hill and R. E. Hoskisson, "Strategy and Structure in the Multiple Firm," *Academy of Management Review* (April 1987): 331–334.

45. D. J. Teece, "Internal Organization and Economic Performance: An Empirical Analysis of Profitability of Principal Firms," *Journal of Industrial Economics* 30 (1981): 173–199.

46. R. Willig, "Technology and Market Structure," *American Economic Review* 69 (1978): 346–351.

47. L. R. Porter, *Competitive Advantage: Creating and Sustaining Superior Performance* (New York: Free Press, 1985).

48. W. Lewellen, "A Pure Financial Rationale for the Conglomerate Merger," *Journal of Finance* 26 (1971): 521–545.

49. B. Baysinger and R. E. Hoskisson, "Diversification Strategy and R&D Intensity in Multiproduct Firms," *Academy of Management Journal* 12 (1989): 310–322.

50. O. E. Williamson, *Corporate Control and Business Behavior* (Englewood Cliffs, N.J.: Prentice-Hall, 1970), p. 134.

51. R. W. Ackerman, "Influences of Integration and Diversity in the Investment Process," *Administrative Science Quarterly* 15 (1976): 341–351.

52. R. A. Armour and D. J. Teece, "Organizational Structure and Economic Performance: A Test of the Multidivisional Hypothesis," *Bell Journal of Economics* 9 (1978): 106–122.

53. B. C. Harris, *Organization, the Effect of Large Corporations* (Ann Arbor, Mich.: UMI Research Press, 1983).

54. R. P. Rumelt, *Strategy, Structure and Economic Performance* (Cambridge, Mass.: Harvard University Press, 1924).

55. E. Mansfield, "How Rapidly Does New Industrial Technology Leak Out," *Journal of Industrial Economics* 14 (1985): 217–225.

56. F. M. Scherer, *Industrial Market Structure and Economic Performance* (Chicago: Rand McNally Co., 1984).

SELECTED BIBLIOGRAPHY

Ackerman, R. W. "Influences of Integration and Diversity in the Investment Process." *Administrative Science Quarterly* 15 (1976): 341–351.

Armour, R. A., and D. J. Teece. "Organizational Structure and Economic Performance: A Test of the Multidivisional Hypothesis." *Bell Journal of Economics* 9 (1978): 106–122.

Astley, W. G. "Sources of Power in Organizational Life." Unpublished Doctoral Dissertation, University of Washington, 1978.

Baiman, Stanley. "Agency Researching Managerial Accounting: A Survey." *Journal of Accounting Literature* (Spring, 1982): 154–213.

Barnard, C. I. *Functions of the Executive*. Cambridge, Mass.: Harvard University Press, 1938.

Baysinger, B., and R. E. Hoskisson. "Diversification Strategy and R&D Intensity in Multiproduct Firms." *Academy of Management Journal* 2, no. 12 (1989): 310–322.

Belkaoui, A., and R. D. Picur. "The Smoothing of Income Numbers: Some Empirical Evidence on Systematic Differences Between Core and Periphery Industrial Sectors." *Accounting, Organizations and Society* (Winter, 1984): 527–545.

Bettis, R. A., and A. Chen. "Organizational Structure and Financial Market Performance: A Preliminary Test." Working paper, Southern Methodist University, Dallas, 1986.

Bourgeois, L. J. "On the Measurement of Organizational Slack." *Academy of Management Review* 6 (1981): 29–39.

Bourgeois, J., and J. V. Singh. "Organizational Slack and Political Behavior within Top Management." *Academy of Management Proceedings* (1983): 43–47.

Buhner, R., and P. Moller. "The Informational Content of Corporate Disclosure of Divisionalization Decisions." *Journal of Management Studies* 22 (1985): 309–326.

Chandler, A. G. *Strategy and Structure: Chapters in the History of the American Industrial Enterprise*. Cambridge, Mass.: M.I.T. Press, 1962.

Cyert, R. M., and J. G. March. *A Behavioral Theory of the Firm*. Englewood Cliffs, N.J.: Prentice-Hall, 1963.

DiMaggio, P., and W. Powell. "Institutional Isomorphism." *American Sociological Review* 48 (1983): 147–160.

Donaldson, L. "The Management of Risk: Structural Portfolio Effects and the M-Form." Working paper, Australian Graduate School of Management, University of New South Wales, Kensington, N.S.W. Australia, 1986.

Dundas, K. N. M., and P. R. Richardson. "Implementing the Unrelated Product Strategy." *Strategic Management Journal* 3 (1982): 287–301.

Eccles, R. G. *The Transfer Pricing Problem: A Theory for Practice*. Lexington, Mass.: Lexington Books, 1985.

Ezzamel, M. A., and K. Hilton. "Divisionalization in British Industry: A Preliminary Study." *Accounting and Business Research* 10 (1980): 197–211.

Fligstein, Neil. "The Spread of the Multidivisional Form Among Large Firms, 1919–1979." *American Sociological Review* (June, 1985): 377–391.

Galbraith, J. R., and D. A. Nathanson. "Role of Organizational Structure and Process in Strategic Implementation." In D. Schendel and C. Hofer, eds., *Strategic Management: A New View of Business Policy and Planning*. Boston: Little, Brown and Co., 1979, pp. 249–283.

Hambrick, D. C., and C. C. Snow. "A Contextual Model of Strategic Decision Making in Organizations." In R. L. Taylor, J. J. O'Connell, R. A. Zawacki, and D. D. Warrick, eds., *Academy of Management Proceedings* (1977): 109–112.

Hannan, M., and J. Freeman. "The Population Ecology of Organizations." *American Journal of Sociology* 92 (1977): 929–946.

———. "Structural Inertia and Organizational Change." *American Sociological Review* 49 (1984): 149–164.

Harrigan, K. R. "Vertical Integration and Corporate Strategy." *Academy of Management Journal* 928 (1985): 397–425.

Harris, B. C. *Organization, The Effect of Large Corporations*. Ann Arbor, Mich.: UMI Research Press, 1983.

Hill, C. W. L. "Internal Organization and Enterprise Performance." *Managerial and Decision Economics* 6 (1985): 210–216.

Hill, C. W. L., and R. E. Hoskisson. "Strategy and Structure in the Multiproduct Firm." *Academy of Management Review* (April 1987): 331–334.

Hoskisson, R. E. "Corporate Growth Strategy and Implementation of the Multidivisional Structure: The Effect on Risk, Return and Growth." *Southwest Academy of Management Proceedings* (1987): 33–37.

———. "Multidivisional Structure and Performance: The Contingency of Diversification Strategy." *Academy of Management Journal* (December 1987): 625–644.

Hoskisson, R. E., and C. S. Galbraith. "The Effect of Quantum Versus Incremental M-Form Reorganization on Performance: A Time-Series Exploration of Intervention Dynamics." *Journal of Management* 11 (1985): 55–70.

Kamin, J. Y., and J. Ronen. "The Smoothing of Income Numbers: Some Empirical Evidence on Systematic Differences Among Management-Controlled and Owner-Controller Firms." *Accounting, Organizations and Society* 3, no. 2 (1978): 141–157.

Kerr, J. L. "Diversification Strategy and Managerial Rewards: An Empirical Study." *Academy of Management Journal* 28 (1978): 155–179.

Lant, T. K. "Modeling Organizational Slack: An Empirical Investigation," Stanford University Research Paper #856, 1986.

Libenstein, H. "X-Efficiency: From Concept to Theory," *Challenge* (September-October 1979): 13–22.

———. "Allocative Efficiency vs. X-Efficiency." *American Economic Review* (June 1966): 392–415.

Levinthal, D., and J. G. March. "A Model of Adaptive Organization Search." *Journal of Economic Behavior and Organization* 15 (1973): 162–180.

Lewellen, W. "A Pure Financial Rationale for the Conglomerate Merger." *Journal of Finance* 26 (1971): 521–545.

Lewin, A. Y., and C. Wolf. "The Theory of Organizational Slack: A Critical Review." *Proceedings: Twentieth International Meeting of TIMS* (1976): 648–654.

Lorsch, J. W., and S. A. Allen. *Managing Diversity and Interdependence*. Boston: Division of Research, Harvard Graduate School of Business Administration, 1973.

Mansfield, E. "How Rapidly Does New Industrial Technology Lead Out." *Journal of Industrial Economics* 34 (1985): 217–225.

March, J. G. "Decisions in Organizations and Theories of Choice." In Andrew H. Van de Ven and William F. Joyce, eds., *Perspectives on Organizational Design and Behavior*. New York: Wiley, 1981.

March, J. G., and H. A. Simon. *Organizations*. New York: Wiley, 1958.

Pfeffer, J. *Power in Organizations*. Marshfield, Mass.: Pitman, 1981.

———. *Organizations and Organizational Theory*. Marshfield, Mass.: Pitman, 1982.

Pfeffer, J., and G. Salancik. *The External Control of Organizations: A Resource Dependency Perspective*. New York: Harper and Row, 1978.

Pondy, L. R. "Organizational Conflict: Concepts and Models." *Administrative Science Quarterly* 12 (1967): 296–320.

Porter, L. R. *Competitive Advantage: Creating and Sustaining Superior Performance*. New York: Free Press, 1985.

Rosner, Martin M. "Economic Determinant of Organizational Innovation." *Administrative Science Quarterly* 12 (1968): 614–625.

Rumelt, R. P. *Strategy, Structure and Economic Performance*. Cambridge, Mass.: Harvard University Press, 1974.

Scherer, F. M. *Industrial Market Structure and Economic Performance*. Chicago: Rand McNally Co., 1984.

Schein, V. E. "Examining an Illusion: The Role of Deceptive Behaviors in Organizations." *Human Relations* 23 (1979): 287–295.

Schiff, M., and A. Y. Lewis. "The Impact of People on Budgets." *The Accounting Review* (April 1970): 259–268.

Simon, H. A. *Administrative Behavior*. New York: Free Press, 1957.

Singh, J. V. "Performance, Slack, and Risk Taking in Organizational Decision Making." *Academy of Management Journal* (September 1986): 562–585.

Steer, P., and J. Cable. "Internal Organization and Profit: An Empirical Analysis of Large U.K. Companies." *Journal of Industrial Economics* 30 (1981): 201–211.

Teece, D. J. "Internal Organization and Economic Performance: An Empirical Analysis of the Profitability of Principal Firms." *Journal of Industrial Economics* 30 (1981): 173–199.

Thompson, J. D. *Organizations in Action*. New York: McGraw-Hill, 1967.

Thompson, R. S. "International Organization and Profit: A Note." *Journal of Industrial Economics* 30 (1981): 201–211.

Williamson, O. E. "A Model of Rational Managerial Behavior." In R. M. Cyert and J. G. March, eds., *A Behavioral Theory of the Firm*. Englewood Cliffs, N.J.: Prentice-Hall, 1963.

———. *The Economy of Discretionary Behavior: Managerial Objectives in the Theory of the Firm*. Englewood Cliffs, N.J.: Prentice-Hall, 1964.

———. *Corporate Control and Business Behavior*. Englewood Cliffs, N.J.: Prentice-Hall, 1970.

Willig, R. *Markets and Hierarchies: Analysis and Anti-Trust Implication*. New York: Free Press, 1975.

———. "Technology and Market Structure." *American Economic Review* 69 (1978): 346–351.

4

Organizational Slack and Performance Plan Adoption

4.1 INTRODUCTION

Recent accounting research has argued that managerial compensation contracts influence managerial decision making[1,2,3,4] and motivate executives to improve firm performance by working harder, lengthening their decision horizons, and becoming less risk-averse in their investment decisions.[5,6,7] The evidence shows that performance plan adoption was associated with an increase in capital expenditures.[8,9] Other related evidence indicates that the adoption of performance plans was associated with (1) a decrease in corporate risk,[10] (2) mixed evidence on the stock market reaction to the announcement of performance plan adoption,[11,12,13] and (3) significant positive excess returns on announcements of mergers and sell-offs by firms with performance plans.[14]

Organizational slack is a cushion of actual resources used by organizations to adapt successfully either to internal pressures for adjustments or to external pressures for changes in policy.[15,16] A review of the concept of organizational slack and its use in theory indicates that there are two measures.[17] Organizational slack is conceptualized as *unabsorbed slack*, which corresponds to the excess, uncommitted resources in organizations. It is also conceptualized as *absorbed slack*, which corresponds to excess costs in organizations.[18] This distinction raises the following question: How does performance plan adoption affect changes in absorbed and unabsorbed slack? The question is investigated here. The empirical results indicate that firms adopting performance plans (relative to similar nonadopting firms) decrease the amount of unabsorbed slack they were holding.

These results make a significant contribution to research for two reasons. First, they demonstrate a relationship between performance plan adoption and unabsorbed slack. It suggests that some of the resources needed for investment following the adoption of performance plans, as shown by D. F. Larcker,[19] come from the organization's unabsorbed slack. Second, they show that the adoption of performance plan is not sufficient to reduce absorbed slack. This means that managers have incentives to invest unused resources, but that the plan is insufficient to get them to give up perks.

The remainder of the chapter consists of four sections. Section 4.2 discusses the theoretical linkages between performance plan adoption and organizational slack. Section 4.3 describes the methodology used. Section 4.4 presents the empirical results. The research findings are discussed and summarized in Section 4.5.

4.2 PERFORMANCE PLANS AND ORGANIZATIONAL SLACK

In essence, organizational slack is the difference between resources available to management and the resources used by management. Management uses it as a buffer to deal with internal as well as external events that may arise and/or threaten an established coalition.[20] The performance plan adoptions motivate management to improve firm performance as evidenced by the increase in capital expenditures reported by Larcker.[21] The resources needed by management for such endeavors can be easily provided by the excess resources of organizational slack. The use of organizational slack may, however, depend on whether the slack is absorbed or unabsorbed.

First, performance plans are based on accounting measures of corporate performance. The adoption of a performance plan will encourage managers to allocate their efforts to the improvement of the short-term accounting performance measure through reduction of costs. Accordingly, absorbed slack, also labeled administrative slack, is expected to decrease following the adoption of performance plan.

Second, the adoption of performance plan will encourage managers to allocate their efforts to the improvement of long-term accounting performance measures by searching for, and spending for, new investment opportunities. Some of the resources needed for the new investment may come from unabsorbed slack. Accordingly, unabsorbed slack is expected to decrease following the adoption of a performance plan.

The following research hypotheses are examined in the subsequent empirical study.

H1: The adoption of a performance plan is associated with decrease in absorbed slack.

H2: The adoption of a performance plan is associated with a decrease in unabsorbed slack.

4.3 METHODS

This study uses a longitudinal design because the relationship between performance plan adoption and organizational slack occurs over time.

4.3.1 Sample and Data Collection

A list of corporate incentive plans was obtained from previous research[22] and through independent historical research. Each experimental firm was required to satisfy two criteria. First, the performance plan adoption must have occurred during the 1971–82 period. Second, a firm passing the first criterion must have a matching control firm.

A total of seventy experimental firms were identified. A sample of companies is given in Exhibit 4.1. The control firms were required to satisfy the following criteria:

1. same industry as the experimental firms[23]
2. similar size as the experimental firm measured by corporate sales in the year prior to performance plan adoption by the experimental firm
3. similar fiscal year as the experimental firm[24]

To measure the effect of the performance plan, organizational slack is analyzed before and after the change while controlling for one categorical variable and two covariates.

4.3.2 Dependent Variables

Financial statement data for years –5 to +5 (relative to the year of adoption of the performance plan by the experimental company) for each firm was collected from Compustat. Year 0, the year of adoption of the performance plan, was excluded from the analysis to avoid confounding the slack measures with outcomes during the transition. The data collected were on absorbed slack and unabsorbed slack.

A two-component concept of slack has been proposed that made the distinction between absorbed slack, referring to slack absorbed as costs in organizations, and unabsorbed slack, referring to uncommitted resources. Analogously, absorbed slack was measured by (1) the ratio of selling, general and administrative expenses to the cost of goods sold in order to capture slack absorbed in salaries, overhead expenses, and various administrative costs, and (2) the ratio of working capital to sales in order to capture the absorption of slack related to capital utilization. Unabsorbed slack was computed as cash plus marketable securities minus current liabilities divided by sales, in order to capture the amount of liquid resources uncommitted to liabilities in the near future.

4.3.3 Control Variable and Covariates

One control variable and two covariates were used to control for possible intervening effects.

Exhibit 4.1
Sample of Companies

Experimental Firm	Year°	Control Firm
A E Staley	1980	Hormel
Akzona	1971	Lowenstein
Allied Corp	1980	Halliburton
AMF	1980	General Tire
Armstrong Rubber	1982	Cooper Tire
Ashland Oil	1979	Standard Oil (Ohio)
Atlantic Richfield	1976	Cities Service
Baxter Travenol	1982	Schering-Plough
Beatrice Foods	1978	Quaker Oats
Bemis	1974	Great Northern Kekoosa
Bendix	1974	Fruehauf
Black & Decker	1980	Baker International
Bristol Myers	1978	Avon Products
Burroughs	1982	Digital Equipment
Cabot	1972	Handy & Harman
Celanese	1980	Hercules
Central Soya	1981	Anderson Clayton
Cincinnati Milacron	1979	Ametek
Combustion Eng.	1978	Gillette
Cooper Labs	1978	I C N Pharma
Corning Glass	1979	Norton
Crown Zellerbach	1973	Diamond International
Datapoint	1979	Storage Technology
Diamond Shamrock	1980	Sherwin Williams
Dover	1974	Harnischfeger
Eaton	1974	Lockheed
Emerson Electric	1977	Whirlpool
Ferro	1982	Syntex
FMC	1973	DuPont
General Mills	1980	Carnation
General Motors	1982	Ford
Hershey Foods	1978	International Multifoods
Hobart	1977	Scott & Fetzer
Honeywell	1978	Litton
Illinois Toolworks	1980	Hornischfeger
International Harvester	1975	Borg Warner
Koopers	1979	Phelps Dodge
Manville	1978	US Gypsum
Merck	1982	Sterling Drug
Minnesota Mining	1981	TRW
Monsanto	1974	Dow Chemical
Nabisco	1976	Campbell Taggert
Nalco	1977	Schering-Plouch

(continued)

Exhibit 4.1   (Continued)

Nashua	1981	Dennison
NCR	1982	Deere
NL Industries	1978	Schlumberger
Outboard Marine	1982	Briggs & Stratton
Owens Corning	1980	Libbey Owens Ford
Owens Illinois	1975	Owens Corning
Phillips Petroleum	1978	Cities Service
Pillsbury	1975	International Multifoods
Ralston-Purina	1975	Carnation
Rexnord	1982	Smith International
Roblin	1977	Midland Ross
Rockwell International	1977	General Dynamics
Sanders Associates	1980	Tracor
Sealed Power	1978	Compugraphic
Shell	1979	Standard Oil (Indiana)
Singer	1981	Martin Marietta
Squibb	1975	Pfizer
Sun Co.	1972	Royal Dutch Petroleum NV
Sybron	1981	Becton Dickinson
Texas Instruments	1980	Raytheon
Textron	1982	Dresser Inc.
Toro	1976	Hesston
Union Oil Co.	1975	Conoco
United Technologies	1979	Boeing
Vulcan Materials	1973	Anchor Hocking
Warner Lambert	1982	American Home Products
Westinghouse	1979	RCA

*Year in which the experimental firm adopted a performance plan.

First, to control for size and profitability, total assets and rate of return on assets were used as covariates.

Second, an influence on the use of slack may have advantages or disadvantages resulting from early or late adoption of performance plans within a set of competitors. Another argument is that imitators may learn from first adopters' mistakes and can benefit from the adoption of performance plans. To control for innovation effects, the experimental firms were coded into two groups, with the first thirty early adopters of performance plans classified as early adopters and the rest as late adopters.

4.3.4 Data Analysis

Analysis of covariance was used to test the overall relationship among (1) slack and firm effect, (2) slack and performance plan adoption, and (3) the interaction of firm effect and performance plan adoption on slack. The model's control variable was early/late adoption and covariates included assets and rate of return on assets.

4.4 RESULTS

Exhibits 4.2, 4.3, and 4.4 present overall results for the two measures of absorbed slack and the measure of unabsorbed slack. Exhibit 4.5 presents the means and standard deviations of each of the slack measures before and after the adoption of the performance plan for both the experimental and control groups of firms.

The first measure of absorbed slack is the ratio of selling, general and administrative expenses as a percentage of cost of goods sold, in order to capture slack absorbed in salaries, overhead expenses, and various administrative costs. The results for this measure of absorbed slack are reported in Exhibit 4.2 and show that the main firm effects and performance plan adoption as well as the interactive effects on slack are both insignificant. The same result is found in Exhibit 4.5 for this measure.

The second measure of absorbed slack is the ratio of working capital to sales, which is used to capture the absorption of slack related to capital utilization. Results regarding this second measure of absorbed slack are summarized in Exhibit 4.3 and show that the main effects of firm effects and performance plan adoption as well as the interaction effects on slack are all insignificant. The same result is found in Exhibit 4.5 for this measure.

Exhibit 4.2
Results of Overall Analysis of Covariance for Absorbed Slack Computed as Selling, General and Administrative Expenses/Cost of Goods Sold°

Sources	F	P
A: Firm Effect (Experimental Control)	1.53	0.2170
B: Performance Plan Adoption (before/after)	0.92	0.3382
A x B interaction	0.89	0.3462
Control Variables:		
Early/Late adoption	21.79	0.0001
Covariate:		
Size	28.27	0.0001
Rate of return on assets	71.87	0.0001

° $R^2 = 0.1607$
Overall F = 20.88 (P = 0.0001)

Exhibit 4.3
Results of Overall Analysis of Covariance for Absorbed Slack Computed as Working Capital/Sales°

Sources	F	P
A: Firm Effect (Experimental Control)	0.13	0.7152
B: Performance Plan Adoption (before/after)	3.19	0.0748
A x B interaction	0.06	0.8093
Control Variables:		
Early/Late adoption	1.58	0.2094
Covariate:		
Size	35.52	0.0001
Rate of return on assets	136.79	0.0001

° $R^2 = 0.2084$
Overall F = 29.54 (P = 0.0001)

The measure of unabsorbed slack is the ratio of cash plus marketable securities minus current liabilities to sales. This measure is used to capture the amount of liquid resources uncommitted to liabilities in the near future. Results regarding this measure of unabsorbed slack are summarized in Exhibit 4.4 and show

Exhibit 4.4
Results of Overall Analysis of Covariance for Unabsorbed Slack Computed as (Cash + Marketable Securities – Current Liabilities)/Sales°

Sources	F	P
A: Firm Effect (Experimental Control)	5.09	0.0245
B: Performance Plan Adoption (before/after)	14.13	0.0002
A x B interaction	4.38	0.0368
Control Variables:		
Early/Late adoption	0.01	0.9217
Covariate:		
Size	7.11	0.0079
Rate of return on assets	165.10	0.0001

° $R^2 = 0.2255$
Overall F = 32.67 (P = 0.0001)

Exhibit 4.5
T Tests and Slack Means by Firm Group before and after Performance Plan Adoption

	Before Adoption	After Adoption	T
Slack 1*			
Experimental Group			
Mean	0.2571	0.30571	1.4962
Control Group			
Mean	0.3216	0.3215	0.0021
Slack 2*			
Experimental Group			
Mean	0.1928	0.21166	1.3015
Control Group			
Mean	0.1992	0.2135	0.9486
Slack 3*			
Experimental Group			
Mean	−0.1181	−0.1236	2.1209
Control Group			
Mean	−0.0713	0.1252	2.9442

that the following relationships are all significant at $\alpha = 0.05$: (1) between slack and firm effect, (2) between slack and performance plan adoption, and (3) between firm effect-performance plan adoption interactions and slack. An examination of the mean results on unabsorbed slack in Exhibit 4.5 shows a significant reduction in unabsorbed slack taking place subsequent to the adoption of the performance plan. This result is consistent with Hypothesis 2. That is, unabsorbed slack declines following the adoption of the performance plan. It suggests that following the implementation of compensation plans managers do seek new investment opportunities as shown in Larcker.[25] It also suggests that some of the resources needed for the new investment come from the unabsorbed slack existing in the firms. The amount of liquid resources uncommitted to liabilities in the near future appears as the first resources to be invested by managers following the adopting of performance plans.

4.5 DISCUSSION AND SUMMARY

The hypothesis that changes in executive compensation contracts are associated with changes in managerial decisions is important to the incentive research taking place in management, accounting, and economic research. One incentive question investigated in this study concerns the association between performance plan adoption and organizational slack. A differentiation was made between absorbed slack and unabsorbed slack. The results on absorbed slack were insignificant. However, the empirical results indicate that, when compared to similar nonadopting firms, those that adopt performance plans exhibit a significant reduction in unabsorbed slack following plan adoption. A logical interpretation is that the performance plan encourages managers to allocate their efforts toward improving accounting-based long-term performance measures by increasing capital investment. That investment leads to a reduction of the unabsorbed slack. The unabsorbed slack is used to fund some of the increase in capital investment.

NOTES

1. R. L. Watts and J. L. Zimmerman, "Towards a Positive Theory of the Determination of Accounting Standards," *The Accounting Review* (January 1978): 112–134.

2. R. L. Hagerman and M. E. Zmijewski, "Some Economic Determinants of Accounting Policy Choice," *Journal of Accounting and Economics* 1 (1979): 141–161.

3. R. Dukes, T. R. Dyckman, and J. Elliot, "Accounting for Research and Development Costs: The Impact on Research and Development Expenditures," *Journal of Accounting Research* 18 (supplement 1981): 1–26.

4. B. Horwitz and R. Kolodny, "The Economic Effects of Involuntary Uniformity in the Financial Reporting of R & D Expenditures," *Journal of Accounting Research* 18 (supplement 1981): 38–74.

5. C. P. Baril, "Long Term Incentive Compensation, Ownership, and the Decision Horizon Problem," Working paper, McIntire School of Commerce, University of Virginia, Charlottesville, 1991.

6. D. F. Larcker, "The Association Between Performance Plan Adoption and Corporate Capital Investment," *Journal of Accounting and Economics* (April 1983): 9–30.

7. C. W. Smith and R. L. Watts, "Incentive and Tax Effects of U.S. Executive Compensation Plans," *Australian Journal of Management* (December 1982): 39–157.

8. Larcker, "The Association Between Performance Plan Adoption and Corporate Capital Investment."

9. J. J. Gaver, K. M. Gaver, and S. Furze, "The Association Between Performance Plan Adoption and Corporate Investment Decisions," Working paper, University of Oregon, 1989.

10. Ibid.

11. J. A. Brickley, S. Bhagat, and R. C. Lease, "The Impact of Long-Range Managerial Compensation Plan on Shareholder Wealth," *Journal of Accounting and Economics* (April 1985): 115–129.

12. J. J. Gaver, K. M. Gaver, and G. P. Battistel, "The Stock Market Reaction to Performance Plan Adoptions," *The Accounting Review* (January 1992): 172–182.

13. R. Kumar and P. R. Sopariwala, "The Effect of Adoption of Long-Term Performance Plans on Stock Prices and Accounting Numbers," Working Paper, Virginia Polytechnic Institute and State University, 1991.

14. H. Tehranian and J. F. Waegelein, "Market Reaction to Short-Term Executive Compensation Plan Adoption," *Journal of Accounting and Economics* (April 1985): 131–144.

15. L. J. Bourgeois, "On the Measurement of Organizational Slack," *Academy of Management Review* (October 1981): 29–39.

16. J. G. March, "Bounded Rationality, Ambiguity, and the Engineering of Choice," *Bell Journal of Economics* 9 (1978): 587–608.

17. J. V. Singh, "Performance, Slack, and Risk Taking in Strategic Decisions: Test of a Structural Equation Model," Unpublished Doctoral dissertation, Graduate School of Business, Stanford University, Palo Alto, Calif., 1983.

18. O. E. Williamson, *The Economics of Discretionary Behavior: Managerial Objectives in a Theory of the Firm* (Englewood Cliffs, N.J.: Prentice-Hall, 1964).

19. Larcker, "The Association Between Performance Plan Adoption and Corporate Capital Investment."

20. R. M. Cyert and J. G. March, *A Behavioral Theory of the Firm* (Englewood Cliffs, N.J.: Prentice-Hall, 1963), p. 36.

21. Larcker, "The Association Between Performance Plan Adoption and Corporate Capital Investment."

22. Ibid.

23. For the seventy matched pairs, forty-six had the same two-digit SIC code, five had the same three-digit SIC code, and nineteen had the same four-digit SIC code.

24. If a firm was a December year-end company, matches were allowed with September through December firms. However, in most cases December experimental firms were matched with December control firms. For non-December firms, a match was allowed with firms whose fiscal year end was close to that of the experimental firm.

25. Larcker, "The Association Between Performance Plan Adoption and Corporate Capital Investment."

SELECTED BIBLIOGRAPHY

Baril, C. P. "Long Term Incentive Compensation, Ownership, and the Decision Horizon Problem." Working paper, McIntire School of Commerce, University of Virginia, Charlottesville, 1988.

Bourgeois, L. J. "On the Measurement of Organizational Slack." *Academy of Management Review* 6 (October 1981): 29–39.

Bourgeois, L. J., and J. V. Singh. "Organizational Slack and Political Behavior Within Top Management Teams." *Academy of Management Proceedings* (1983): 43–47.

Brickley, J. A., S. Bhagat, and R. C. Lease. "The Impact of Long-Range Managerial Compensation Plans on Shareholder Wealth." *Journal of Accounting and Economics* 7 (April 1985): 115–29.

Dukes, R., T. R. Dyckman, and J. Elliot. "Accounting for Research and Development Costs: The Impact on Research and Development Expenditures." *Journal of Accounting Research* 18 (supplement, 1981): 1–26.

Gaver, J. J., K. M. Gaver, and G. P. Battistel. "The Stock Market Reaction to Performance Plan Adoptions." *The Accounting Review* 1 (January 1992): 172–182.

Gaver, J. J., K. M. Gaver, and S. Furze. "The Association Between Performance Plan Adoption and Corporate Investment Decisions." Working paper, University of Oregon, 1989.

Hagerman, R. L., and M. E. Zmijewski. "Some Economic Determinants of Accounting Policy Choice." *Journal of Accounting and Economics* 1 (1979): 141–161.

Horwitz, B., and R. Kolodny. "The Economic Effects of Involuntary Uniformity in the Financial Reporting of R & D Expenditures." *Journal of Accounting Research* 18 (supplement, 1981): 38–74.

Kumar, R., and P. R. Sopariwala. "The Effect of Adoption of Long-Term Performance Plans on Stock Prices and Accounting Numbers." Working paper, Virginia Polytechnic Institute and State University, 1991.

Larcker, D. F. "The Association Between Performance Plan Adoption and Corporate Capital Investment." *Journal of Accounting and Economics* 5 (April 1983): 9–30.

March, J. G. "Bounded Rationality, Ambiguity, and the Engineering of Choice." *Bell Journal of Economics* 9 (1978): 587–608.

Singh, J. V. *Performance, Slack, and Risk Taking in Strategic Decisions: Test of a Structural Equation Model.* Unpublished doctoral dissertation, Graduate School of Business, Stanford University, Palo Alto, Calif., 1983.

———. "Performance, Slack, and Risk Taking in Organizational Decision Making." *Academy of Management Journal* 3 (September 1986): 562–585.

Smith, C. W., and R. L. Watts. "Incentive and Tax Effects of U.S. Executive Compensation Plans." *Australian Journal of Management* 7 (December 1982): 39–157.

Tehranian, H., and J. F. Waegelein. "Market Reaction to Short-Term Executive Compensation Plan Adoption." *Journal of Accounting and Economics* 7 (April 1985): 131–144.

Watts, R. L., and J. L. Zimmerman. "Towards a Positive Theory of the Determination of Accounting Standards." *The Accounting Review* (January 1978): 112–134.

Williamson, O. E. *The Economics of Discretionary Behavior: Managerial Objectives in a Theory of the Firm.* Englewood Cliffs, N.J.: Prentice-Hall, 1964.

5

Slack Budgeting, Information Distortion, and Self-Esteem

5.1 INTRODUCTION

Psychological variables are very helpful in explaining some of the accountant's behavioral patterns and can contribute to the development of better management accounting systems.[1,2] Personality traits and behavioral factors may be indicative of different accounting behavior and effectiveness. For example, self-disclosure was found to be positively related to attitudes to responsibility accounting[3] and Gordon's Personality Profile and the Ohio State Leadership Behavior Description Questionnaire were found to be a predictor of budgeting behavior.[4,5] Slack creation is another important managerial behavior in need of explanation, correction, and/or control. An evaluation of the effectiveness of a firm's control system requires, among other things, the identification of the behavioral factors that lead to slack creation.[6] Accordingly, this chapter reports on research designed to provide insights into the relationships between the individual characteristics and slack creation. More specifically, it examines slack budgeting as a case of information distortion and investigates empirically the effects of self-esteem feedback on information distortion.

5.2 THEORY

5.2.1 Slack Budgeting and Information Distortion

The literature on the behavioral implications of budgets as instruments of planning and control has found its way into most cost accounting textbooks.[7] It is suggested that the budget in its dual role of being a planning tool and a control device may give rise to slack. Cyert and March[8] defined organizational slack as the difference between "the total resources available to the firm and the total necessary to maintain the organizational coalition." Slack arises from imperfections in the organizational process of resource allocation. Slack may be distributed in the form of additional dividends and excessive wages beyond the minimum required to obtain a healthy coalition of all the participants in the organization or may be undistributed as idle cash and securities. In examining the relationships between the controller and the controlled within the organization, Schiff and Lewin[9] argued that these relationships revolved around the budget process and that the "controlled" exercise significant influence on the outcome of the budgets by the incorporation of slack into their budgets.[10] In brief, because the budget is an expression of the performance criteria and because managers bargain and participate in its formation, the budget process may become the vehicle for slack. Thus, organizational slack is a general organizational phenomenon that may be reflected in slack budgeting behavior. In an accounting framework, slack budgeting is, in general, operationally defined as the process of understating revenues and overstating costs. Lowe and Shaw[11] report also on downward and upward bias introduced in sales forecasts by line managers, which may indicate the existence of negative slack in some cases.

Slack creation is a generalized organizational phenomenon. Various organizational factors have been used to explain slack creation, namely organizational structure, goal congruence, control system, and managerial behavior. Basically, (1) it is assumed to occur in cases where a Tayloristic organization structure exists,[12] although it is also assumed to occur in a participative organization structure;[13] (2) it may be due to conflicts arising between the individual and organizational goals leading managers to intentionally create slack;[14,15] (3) it may be due to the attitudes of management toward the budget and to the workers' views of budgets as devices used by management to manipulate them; and (4) it may occur whether or not the organization is based on a centralized or decentralized structure.

Whatever the sources or causes of slack creation, slack involves a deliberate distortion of input information. Distortion of input information in a budget setting in particular arises from a need by managers to accommodate their expectations about the kinds of payoff associated with different possible outcomes. For example, Cyert, March, and Starbuck[16] (hereafter referred to as CMS) showed in a laboratory experiment that subjects adjusted the information they transmitted in a complex decision making system to control their payoffs. Similarly, Lowe and Shaw[17] have shown that in cases where rewards were related to forecast, sales managers tended to distort the input information and to induce biases in their sales forecast. Dalton[18] also provided some rich situational descriptions of information distortion in which lower level managers distorted the budget information and allocated resources to what was perceived to be justifiable objectives. Finally, given the existence of a payoff structure that may induce a forecaster to intentionally bias his forecast, Barefield[19] provides a model of forecast behavior that shows a "rough" formulation of a possible link between a forecaster's biasing and the quality of the forecaster as a source of data for an accounting system. All these studies seem to suggest that slack budgeting through systematic distortion of input information may be used to accommodate the subject's expectations about the payoffs associated with various possible outcomes. They fail, however, to provide a better rationalization of the link between distortion of input information and the subject's accommodation of their expectations. Agency theory and risk aversion related issues may provide such a link. Hence, given the existence of divergent incentives and information asymmetry between controller (or employer) and controllee (or employee) and the high cost of observing employee skill or effort, a budget-based employment contract (i.e., employee compensation is contingent on meeting the performance standard) can be Pareto superior to fixed pay or linear sharing rules (where the employer and employee split the output).[20] However, these budget-based schemes impose a risk on the employee (because job performance may be affected by a host of uncontrollable factors). Consequently, risk-averse individuals may resort to slack budgeting through systematic distortion of input information. Moreover, any enhanced (increased) risk aversion would, in practice, lead the employee to resort to slack budgeting.

5.2.2 Self-Esteem

The enhancement of risk aversion and the resulting distortion of input information may be more pronounced when self-esteem is threatened. It was found that persons who have low opinions of themselves are more likely to cheat than persons with high self-esteem.[21] A situation of dissonance was created in an experimental group by giving out positive feedback about a personality test to some participants and negative feedback to others. Then, all the participants were asked to take part in a competitive game of cards. The participants who received a blow to their self-esteem cheated more than those who had received positive feedback about themselves. Could it also be concluded that slack budgeting through information distortion may be a form of dishonest behavior arising from enhancement of risk aversion caused by a negative feedback on self-esteem? A person's expectations may be an important determinant of his behavior. A negative feedback on self-esteem may lead an individual to develop an expectation of poor performance. At the same time, the individual who is given negative feedback about his self-esteem would be more risk averse than others and would be ready to resort to any behavior to cover the situation. Consequently, he may attempt to distort the input information in order to have an attainable budget. Accordingly, one hypothesis may be stated as follows: *Individuals given negative feedback about their self-esteem will introduce more bias into estimates than individuals given positive or neutral feedback about their self-esteem.*

5.3 METHOD

A laboratory experiment was used to investigate the impact of self-esteem feedback on input information distortion in a budgeting task. The subjects were sixty male and female students drawn from the fourth-year undergraduate accounting theory class, the second-year graduate managerial accounting class, and the introductory undergraduate accounting class in the Faculty of Administration at the University of Ottawa who agreed to cooperate and participate in the experiment. Students rather than managers were used in order to better isolate the impact of self-esteem on input information distortion, given that managers may be influenced by a host of other organizational factors to create slack. The subjects were told that they were participating in a study concerned with the correlation between self-esteem scores and "estimation aptitudes." They were told that the Tennessee Self-Concept Scale (TSCS) would be used to measure their self-esteem, and the "estimation aptitudes" would be ascertained upon the completion of a budgeting test.[22]

All subjects were given the TSCS, and were informed of its nature and intent. The test belongs to a wide variety of instruments that have been employed to measure the self-concept. The instrument is simple for the subject to understand, which explains its popularity as a means of studying and understanding human behavior. Sociologists, psychiatrists, theologians, philosophers, educators, and psychologists have increasingly come to view the self-concept as a central construct for the understanding of people and their behavior. Consequently, a whole theoretical school, known as self-theory, has evolved as evidenced by works of people such as C. R. Rogers,[23] D. Snygg and A. W. Combs,[24] P. Lecky,[25] R. C. Wylie,[26] and others. Self-theory is strongly phenomenological in nature and is based on the general principle that man reacts to his phenomenal world in terms of the way he perceives this world. Self-theory holds that human behavior is always meaningful and that we understand each person's behavior only if we can perceive his phenomenal world as he does. The TSCS was devised for the purpose of measuring the self-concept. Although subject to the limitations of any verbal or pencil and paper type scale, the TSCS is nevertheless applicable to a broad range of people and situations.[27,28,29,30,31,32,33] It yields a number of measures and scores and is well standardized. Among these scores are

1. *The self-criticism score (SC):* High scores indicate a normal, healthy openness and capacity for self-criticism.

2. *The positive score (S):* Scores on ninety items are summed to provide a total *P* score that reflects general esteem. In general, people with high scores tend to like themselves, feel that they are persons of value and worth, have confidence in themselves and act accordingly. People with low scores are doubtful about their own worth, unhappy and have little faith or confidence in themselves.[34]

Other scores are provided by the TSCS. To avoid any confusion, only the positive score is used in this study. The subjects were provided with sufficient information about the TSCS and the positive score to consider it relevant and important.

A week after the administration of the TSCS and before participation in a budgeting paper-and-pencil test, subjects were assigned to one of three experimental conditions: positive, neutral, and negative feedback on self-esteem scores. This manipulation of self-esteem was done by disclosing the highest, lowest, and average scores in the class and by (1) communicating the right score, (2) having the subject's score equal to the highest score in the class, or (3) having the subject's score equal to the lowest score in the class. In general, the first alternative was communicated to those whose right score was around the average score in the class, the second alternative to those with low scores, and the third alternative to those with high scores. The last two alternatives were aimed at temporarily inducing either an increase in self-esteem or a decrease in self-esteem. *The first alternative where no change in self-esteem was sought was intended to be for control purposes.*[35]

The highest scores were 405 for the positive score and 46 for the self-criticism score. The lowest scores were 261 for the positive score and 23 for the self-criticism score. The average scores were 310 for the positive score and 32 for the self-criticism score. The provision of such a range of scores for the false feedback groups was assumed to be high enough to generate a blow to the self-esteem of the subjects.[36] To avoid any confusion the subjects were provided only with the positive scores.

The experimental material included four pages: one page for instructions; one page for the positive, neutral, or negative feedback on their self-esteem scores; and the last two pages for a paper-and-pencil test requiring the subject to make cost and sales estimates.

The instructions stated

> The purpose of this experiment is to correlate the estimation ability with self-esteem characteristics. In order to get a true measure of a person's estimation ability, it is necessary to keep in mind the estimation's objective function, which is first, to ensure that the budget is *attainable* and, second, that the budget is *accurate*. In order to accomplish this, I am having you engage in the estimation of both cost and sales for a fictional situation. It is important that you keep the estimation's objective function in mind when making your decision. The second page gives your self-esteem score. The last two pages constitute the budgeting situation.

The second page for the feedback on the self-esteem scores stated: "In the middle of the semester, you were asked to complete the Tennessee Self-Concept Scale. The test belongs to a wide variety of instruments that have been employed to measure the self-concept. The test gives a measure of self-esteem. Persons with high scores tend to like themselves, feel that they are persons of value and worth, have confidence in themselves, and act accordingly. Your score was ___. The highest score, the lowest, and the average scores in your class were respectively ___, ___, ___."

The last two pages of the experimental material included a paper-and-pencil budgeting test requiring each subject to make ten estimates on the basis of the estimates of others. Two versions of the budgeting test were presented: a cost version and a sales version. The cost version reads as follows: "Assume that you are the controller of a manufacturing company considering the production of a new product. You are required to submit your estimate of the unit cost of the product if 500,000 units are produced. Your two assistants A and B, in whom you have equal confidence, presented you with preliminary estimates. For each of the cases below, indicate your estimate of costs you would submit." The sales version reads as follows: "Assume that you are the marketing manager of a manufacturing concern considering the production of a new product. You are required to submit your estimate of the sales volume of the product if the price is set at $10.80. Your two assistants A and B, in whom you have equal confidence, presented you with preliminary estimates. For each of the cases below, indicate what estimates of sales you would submit."

Each question was followed by a list of ten pairs of numbers, representing the ten pairs of estimates by the two subordinates. The experiment involved in each case the choice between two estimates of cost and two estimates of sales. The cost estimates are indicated in Exhibit 5.1.

The sales estimates were similar in value except that the cost estimates are expressed in dollars and those for sales in units. However, the sales estimates were presented in various different orders to obscure the similarities in values. One such order of sales estimates is indicated in Exhibit 5.2. The three types of feedback on self-esteem scores (negative, neutral, and positive) and the two types of budgeting decisions (cost and sales estimates) resulted in the $2 \times 3 \times N$ factorial design in Exhibit 5.3. The group receiving the correct and hence neutral feedback was intended to be the control group in this experiment.

Exhibit 5.1
Cost Estimates Presented to Participants

Cases	A's estimate	B's estimate	Your estimate
(1)	$1.54	$6.75	$ _____
(2)	$8.42	$4.56	$ _____
(3)	$3.25	$7.52	$ _____
(4)	$1.25	$4.35	$ _____
(5)	$6.54	$4.70	$ _____
(6)	$1.80	$7.30	$ _____
(7)	$6.89	$1.65	$ _____
(8)	$3.25	$7.52	$ _____
(9)	$4.74	$1.54	$ _____
(10)	$3.20	$5.35	$ _____

Exhibit 5.2
Sales Estimates Presented to Participants

Cases	A's estimate	B's estimate	Your estimate
(1)	320,000 units	535,000 units	_____units
(2)	474,000	154,000	_____
(3)	325,000	752,000	_____
(4)	689,000	165,000	_____
(5)	180,000	730,000	_____
(6)	654,000	470,000	_____
(7)	125,000	435,000	_____
(8)	325,000	752,000	_____
(9)	842,000	456,000	_____
(10)	154,000	675,000	_____

The nature of the task is assumed to lead the subjects to build in slack. First, it asks for an attainable budget. Second, the courses being taken by the subjects and taught by the experimenter emphasize the notion of a biased payoff schedule within an organization. Therefore, if the payoffs are perceived to be biased or if they are perceived to depend on considerations other than the relations between the estimate and the true value, the tactical decision on biasing the estimate becomes important to the estimator.

5.4 RESULTS

Each subject's cost and sales estimates E were transformed into a summary statistic x, which represented the weight assigned to the larger of the two given numbers in the pair presented to the subject such that

Exhibit 5.3
Diagram of the Two-Factor Sample Experiment

		Types of feedback sample experiment		
		Negative	Correct	Positive
Types of budgeting	Cost	n = 20	n = 20	n = 20
decisions	Sales	n = 20	n = 20	n = 20

$$E = xU + (1-x)L$$

where U is the upper number and L the lower number.

Upper and lower limits of the 10 pairs ranged from 125 to 842 and included two pairs in which the difference was approximately 200, two pairs in which the difference was approximately 300, two pairs in which the difference was approximately 400, two pairs in which the difference was approximately 550, one pair in which the difference was 521, and one pair in which the difference was 386.

The use of a linear combination of the two estimates was considered superior to a single reliance on the mean. In effect, the summary statistic x highlights the bias brought by the subject to his estimates better than a single use of the mean estimate. It is used in the study as the data base for the analysis of variance. The mean estimate does not highlight the bias because it gives equal weight to the observations.

The analysis of variance is summarized in Exhibit 5.4. The main effects were significant. The nature of the feedback on self-esteem had an impact on the

Exhibit 5.4
Summary ANOVA for Main and Simple Effects

Source of variation	SS	Y	MS	F
A (Budgeting decision)	0.68	1	0.68	5.71*
A for b_1 (negative Feedback) #	(1.690)**(1)		(1.690)	(14.2)*
A for b_2 (neutral feedback)	(0.115)	(1)	(0.115)	(0.9)
A for b_3 (positive feedback)	(0.221)	(1)	(.0221)	(1.01)
B (feedback on self-esteem)	1.6	2	0.8	6.71*
B for a_1 (cost decision)	(0.546)	(2)	(0.273)	(2.29)
B for a_2 (sales decision)	(0.955)	(2)	(0.473)	(3.9)
AB	1.336	2	0.668	5.44*
Within cell	6.474	54	0.119	
Total	10.090	59		

° Significant at .05 level
°° Data for simple effects are between parentheses
Legend: SS = Sum of Squares
       Y = Degrees of freedom
      MS = mean square
      F = F statistic

Exhibit 5.5
Means of Cells Summary Table

	Negative feedback	Neutral feedback	Positive feedback
Cost	0.81	0.50	0.75
Sales	0.23	0.65	0.54

weight assigned to the largest estimate, $F_{obs} = 6.71 > F_{0.95}(2, 54) = 3.20$, and the nature of the budgeting decision had an impact on the weight assigned by the subject to the highest estimate, $F_{obs} = 5.71 > F_{0.95}(1, 54) = 4.00$. The interaction effects were also significant, $F_{obs} = 5.44 > F_{0.95}(1, 54) = 3.20$. The nature of the interaction effects is indicated by an inspection of the cell means. These means are shown in Exhibit 5.5. A geometric representation of these means is also given in Figure 5.1. This figure presents the profiles corresponding to the simple main effects of the type of feedback on self-esteem for each of the budgeting decisions. A response of 0.5 is unbiased and responses of >0.5 for cost estimates and <.05 for sales estimates represent slack creation. The profiles for the cost and sales decisions appear to have different slopes indicating an analysis of the simple effects is warranted. Only one simple effect is significant. Given negative feedback on self-esteem, the impact of the budgeting decision on the weights assigned to the highest estimate is different, $F_{obs} = 14.2 > F_{0.95}(1, 54) =$

Figure 5.1
Profiles of Simple Effects of Feedback on Self-Esteem (mean weight assigned to the highest estimate)

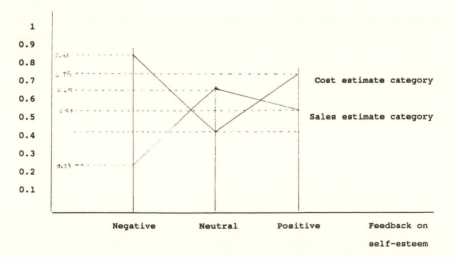

4.00. In fact, in the case of negative feedback, thirteen of the cost response points were superior to 0.5 and fourteen of the sales response points were inferior to 0.5.

However, the experimental data do not indicate a difference in the weights assigned given a neutral (F_{obs} = 0.9) or positive (F_{obs} = 1.01) feedback on self-esteem. *Although the results are not significant, the positive feedback caused slack to be incorporated with cost estimation.* If the positive feedback were significant, the evidence in this study would have been consistent with a curvilinear hypothesis that invalid feedback on self-esteem causes the incorporation of slack. Given the results of this study, however, the evidence seems more consistent with the linear hypothesis that negative feedback on self-esteem causes the incorporation of slack.

5.5 DISCUSSION

These results suggest that inaccurate but neutral or positive feedback on self-esteem may not result in observed differences in the cost or sales budgeting decisions. An inaccurate but favorable feedback on self-esteem does not seem to lead to slack budgeting behavior and distortion of input information. Similarly, negative but inaccurate feedback does lead to a difference in the type of budgeting decision, cost or sale. The inaccurate and negative feedback of self-esteem seems to result in the distortion of input information. An examination of Figure 5.1 shows that given negative feedback on self-esteem, subjects tend to overestimate cost and underestimate sales.

These results seem to support the findings of CMS in part. They support the same idea that cost and sales would tend to be estimated with a bias even though the bias might be in a different direction for each type of estimate. They also support their main proposition that estimates within a complex decision-making system involve attempts by the estimators to control their payoffs. Two differences arise, however, when comparing the scope of both results. First, the differences in the cost and sales estimation decisions result, in our study, in the creation of slack. Our subjects tend to overestimate cost and underestimate sales. Second, our results show that the bias introduced by the estimators is caused by the inaccurate and negative feedback on self-esteem.

One possible interpretation consistent with the observed effect may be related to the cognitive dissonance theory. Inaccurate and negative feedback on self-esteem may lead to enhanced risk aversion and increased dissonance, and because dissonance and risk aversion lead to an effort to reduce them, and because the only means of reduction in this experiment is the budget, slack budgeting behavior is expected.[37]

Another possible interpretation is that slack budgeting behavior occurs as a result of being consistent with an enhanced risk aversion due to a negative self-concept. The inaccurate and negative feedback on self-esteem apparently accentuates the risk aversion leading to a distortion of input information. In other words, a shock to one's self-esteem will cause one to be willing to be a party to cheating to achieve success. Given the nature of the task, the behavior is similar to that which would be exhibited by an increase in one's risk aversion. Two cautions to qualify this conclusion are necessary. First, this study did not assess risk aversion directly and, therefore, one cannot infer from the analysis that individuals with negative feedback on self-esteem are indeed risk averters. Second, future research should incorporate an incentive scheme, otherwise the effects in the negative case may be overstated.

To be consistent with the work of Rogers,[38] the slack budgeting behavior may be altered by first changing the self-concept in a positive direction and thereby reducing the risk aversion. Clearly, any planning or control system within a firm must take into account the predisposition and biases created in the planner by the nature of the feedback on his performance and consequently on his self-esteem: an inaccurate and negative feedback on self-esteem may induce slack. Therefore, the control of slack during the budget-setting period should be emphasized in the case of those employees who previously received an invalid feedback on their performance and self-esteem. In short, if an individual in an organization is tempted to use slack budgeting, it may be easier for him to yield to his temptation if his self-esteem has been lowered by inaccurate negative feedback. It is, however, appropriate to caution that the suggestions derived from the findings are tentative pending replication and further demonstrations of the external validity of this experiment.

One possible improvement would be to investigate whether the results of this study are due solely to the effects of negative and positive feedback on the subjects or are due to their perceived level of self-esteem. A second possible improvement would be to investigate the effects on estimation of accurate information concerning high and low self-esteem. To do so, the experiment should include individuals with high and low levels of self-esteem who either receive no feedback concerning their self-esteem levels (additional control group) or who receive accurate feedback concerning their self-esteem (additional experimental group).

Another possible improvement would be to design an experiment dealing with more than the two budgetary items examined in this experiment, namely cost and sales volume.

5.6 CONCLUSION

Certain hypotheses on slack budgeting were deduced from an examination of the nature of the feedback of self-esteem on the distortion of input information. Three main results appear. First, it can be said that the nature of the feedback on self-esteem has an impact on organizational estimation decisions. Second, the experiment also indicates that the nature of the budgeting decision leads to a different estimation figure. Finally, the negative and inaccurate feedback of self-esteem appears to accentuate the distortion of input information and the creation of slack. Until the impact of accurate feedback of self-esteem is investigated, this study's findings indicate that negative feedback should not be released before it has been categorically proven to be accurate.

NOTES

1. Ahmed Riahi-Belkaoui, *The New Foundations of Management Accounting* (Westport, Conn.: Quorum, 1992).

2. F. Collins, "Managerial Accounting Systems and Organizational Control: A Role Perspective," *Accounting, Organizations and Society* (May 1982): 107–122.

3. Ahmed Belkaoui, "The Relationship Between Self-Disclosure Style and Attitudes to Responsibility Accounting," *Accounting Organizations and Society* (December 1981): 281–289.

4. R. J. Swieringa and R. H. Moncur, "The Relationship Between Managers' Budget Oriented Behavior and Selected Attitudes, Position, Size and Performance Measures," *Empirical Research Studies: Selected Studies, 1972, Journal of Accounting Research* 10 (supplement, 1972): 19.

5. A. G. Hopwood, "An Empirical Study of the Role of Accounting Data in Performance Evaluation," *Empirical Research Studies: Selected Studies 1972, Journal of Accounting Research* 10 (supplement, 1972): 149–209.

6. M. Onsi, "Factor Analysis of Behavioral Variables Affecting Budgetary Slack," *The Accounting Review* (July 1973): 535.

7. Ahmed Riahi-Belkaoui, *Handbook of Cost Accounting* (Westport, Conn.: Quorum, 1992).

8. R. M. Cyert and J. G. March, *A Behavioral Theory of the Firm* (Englewood Cliffs, N.J.: Prentice-Hall, 1963), p. 36.

9. M. Schiff and A. Y. Lewin, "The Impact of People on Budgets," *The Accounting Review* (April 1970): 259–268.

10. Various organizational processes grounded in the development and maintenance of coalitions as well as a variety of group and political behaviors may constitute other cases where those relationships may be either successfully resolved or not.

11. A. E. Lowe and R. W. Shaw, "An Analysis of Managerial Biasing: Evidence from a Company's Budgeting Process," *The Journal of Management Studies* (October 1968): 304–315.

12. C. Argyris, *The Impact of Budgets on People* (New York: The Controllership Foundation, 1952), p. 85.

13. E. H. Caplan, *Management Accounting and Behavioral Sciences* (Reading, Mass.: Addison-Wesley, 1971), p. 85.

14. J. G. March and H. A. Simon, *Organizations* (New York: John Wiley, 1958), p. 84.

15. L. D. Parker, "Goal Congruence: A Misguided Concept," *ABACUS* (June 1976): 12.

16. R. M. Cyert, J. G. March, and W. H. Starbuck, "Two Experiments on Bias and Conflict in Organizational Estimation," *Management Science* (April 1961): 254–264.

17. Lowe and Shaw, "An Analysis of Managerial Biasing: Evidence from a Company's Budgeting Process."

18. M. Dalton, *Men Who Manage* (New York: John Wiley, 1961).

19. R. M. Barefield, "A Model of Forecast Biasing Behavior," *The Accounting Review* (July 1970): 490–501.

20. J. S. Demski and G. A. Feltham, "Economic Incentives in Budgetary Control Systems," *The Accounting Review* (April 1978): 336–359.

21. E. Aronson and D. R. Mettee, "Dishonest Behavior as a Function of Differential Levels of Induced Self-Esteem," *Journal of Personality and Social Psychology* (January 1968): 121–127.

22. W. F. Fitts, *Manual for the Tennessee Self-Concept Scale* (Nashville, Tenn.: Counselor Recording and Tests, 1970).

23. C. R. Rogers, *Client Centered Therapy* (Boston: Houghton Mifflin, 1951).

24. D. Snygg and A. W. Combs, *Individual Behavior* (New York: Harper and Row, 1949).

25. P. Lecky, *Self-Consistency* (New York: Island Press, 1945).

26. R. C. Wylie, *The Self-Concept: A Critical Survey of Pertinent Research Literature* (Lincoln: University of Nebraska Press, 1961).

27. W. F. Fitts, *The Self-Concept and Behavior: Overview and Supplement* (Nashville, Tenn.: Counselor Recording and Tests, 1972).

28. W. F. Fitts, *The Self-Concept and Performance* (Nashville, Tenn.: Counselor Recording and Tests, 1972).

29. W. F. Fitts, *The Self-Concept and Psychopathology* (Nashville, Tenn.: Counselor Recording and Tests, 1972).

30. W. F. Fitts, J. L. Adams, G. Radford, W. C. Richard, B. K. Thomas, M. M. Thomas, and W. Thompson, *The Self-Concept and Self-Actualization* (Nashville, Tenn.: Counselor Recording and Tests, 1971).

31. W. Thomson, *Correlates of the Self-Concept* (Nashville, Tenn.: Counselor Recording and Tests, 1972).

32. W. F. Fitts and W. T. Hammer, *The Self-Concept and Delinquency* (Nashville, Tenn.: Counselor Recording and Tests, 1969).

33. W. F. Fitts, *Interpersonal Competence: The Wheel Model* (Nashville, Tenn.: Counselor Recording and Tests, 1970).

34. Fitts, *Manual for the Tennessee Self-Concept Scale*, p. 1.

35. Parametric and nonparametric tests ($\alpha = 0.10$) failed to reject the hypothesis of no differences in the TSCS scores of the three types of subjects (four-year undergraduate, first-year undergraduate, and second-year graduate).

36. At the end of the experiment the subjects were debriefed and given their correct TSCS scores.

37. In other words, to reduce the risk aversion and to reach more consonance, subjects reverted to a slack budgeting behavior.

38. C. R. Rogers, *Client Centered Therapy* (Boston: Houghton Mifflin, 1951).

SELECTED BIBLIOGRAPHY

Argyris, C. *The Impact of Budgets on People*. New York: The Controllership Foundation, 1952.

Aronson, E., and D. R. Mettee. "Dishonest Behavior as a Function of Differential Levels of Induced Self-Esteem." *Journal of Personality and Social Psychology* (January 1968): 121–127.

Barefield, R. M. "A Model of Forecast Biasing Behavior." *The Accounting Review* (July 1970): 490–501.

Belkaoui, A. *Conceptual Foundations of Management Accounting.* Reading, Mass.: Addison-Wesley, 1980.

―――. "The Relationships Between Self-Disclosure Style and Attitudes to Responsibility Accounting." *Accounting, Organizations and Society* (December 1981): 281–289.

―――. *Cost Accounting: A Multidimensional Emphasis.* Hinsdale, Ill.: Dryden Press, 1983.

Caplan, E. H. *Management Accounting and Behavioral Sciences.* Reading, Mass.: Addison-Wesley, 1971.

Collins, R. "Managerial Accounting Systems and Organizational Control: A Role Perspective." *Accounting Organizations and Society* (May 1982): 107–122.

Cyert, R. M. and J. G. March. *A Behavioral Theory of the Firm.* Englewood Cliffs, N.J.: Prentice-Hall, 1963.

Cyert, R. M., J. G. March, and W. H. Starbuck. "Two Experiments on Bias and Conflict in Organizational Estimation." *Management Science* (April 1961): 254–264.

Dalton, M. *Men Who Manage.* New York: John Wiley, 1961.

Demski, J. S., and G. A. Feltham. "Economic Incentives in Budgetary Control Systems." *The Accounting Review* (April 1978): 336–359.

Fitts, W. F. *Manual for the Tennessee Self-Concept Scale.* Nashville, Tenn.: Counselor Recording and Tests, 1965.

―――. *Interpersonal Competence: The Wheel Model.* Nashville, Tenn.: Counselor Recording and Tests, 1970.

―――. *The Self-Concept and Behavior: Overview and Supplement.* Nashville, Tenn.: Couselor Recording and Tests, 1972a.

―――. *The Self-Concept and Performance.* Nashville, Tenn.: Counselor Recording and Tests, 1972b.

―――. *The Self-Concept and Psychopathology.* Nashville, Tenn.: Counselor Recording and Tests, 1972c.

Fitts, W. F., J. L. Adams, G. Radford, W. C. Richard, B. K. Thomas, M. M. Thomas, and W. Thompson. *The Self-Concept and Self-Actualization.* Nashville, Tenn.: Counselor Recording and Tests, 1971.

Fitts, W. F., and W. T. Hammer. *The Self-Concept and Delinquency.* Nashville, Tenn.: Counselor Recording and Tests, 1969.

Hopwood, A. G. "An Empirical Study of the Role of Accounting Data in Performance Evaluation." *Empirical Research Studies: Selected Studies 1972, Journal of Accounting Research* 10 (supplement, 1972): 194–209.

Lecky, P. *Self-Consistency.* New York: Island Press, 1945.

Love, A. E., and R. W. Shaw. "An Analysis of Managerial Biasing: Evidence from a Company's Budgeting Process." *The Journal of Management Studies* (October 1968): 304–315.

March, J. G., and H. A. Simon. *Organizations.* New York: John Wiley, 1958.

Onsi, M. "Factor Analysis of Behavioral Variables Affecting Budgetary Slack." *The Accounting Review* (July 1973): 535–548.

Parker, L. D. "Goal Congruence: A Misguided Accounting Concept," *ABACUS* (June 1976): 3–13.

Rogers, C. R. *Client Centered Therapy.* Boston: Houghton Mifflin, 1951.

Schiff, M., and A. Y. Lewin. "The Impact of People on Budgets." *The Accounting Review* (April 1970): 259–268.

Snygg, D., and A. W. Combs. *Individual Behavior*. New York: Harper and Row, 1949.

Swieringa, R. J., and R. H. Moncur. "The Relationship Between Managers' Budget Oriented Behavior and Selected Attitudes, Position, Size and Performance Measures." *Empirical Research Studies: Selected Studies, 1972, Journal of Accounting Research* 10 (supplement, 1972): 19.

Thompson, W. *Correlates of the Self-concept*. Nashville, Tenn.: Counselor Recording and Tests, 1972.

Williamson, O. E. *The Economy of Discretionary Behavior: Managerial Objectives in the Theory of the Firm*. Englewood Cliffs, N.J.: Prentice-Hall, 1964.

Wylie, R. C. *The Self-Concept: A Critical Survey of Pertinent Research Literature*. Lincoln: University of Nebraska Press, 1961.

6

Slack Budgeting and Information Distortion: The Impact of Accountability and Self-Monitoring

6.1 INTRODUCTION

Various research has examined opportunistic behavior that is engaged in for purposes of self-interest maximization.[1] Information management, involving distortion, withholding, and/or filtering of certain types of information, emerges as a frequent tactic.[2,3,4] An area where the distortion of information often occurs is the budgeting process leading to the phenomenon of slack budgeting. Initial efforts have been made to identify some of the personal and situational characteristics that encourage the use of slack budgeting to distort information input in the budgeting process.[5,6] Knowledge of the impact of these characteristics can be useful in the management and/or control of slack budgeting, a desirable goal in all types of organizations. More concerted research is needed to explore this issue. Accordingly, the present study addresses the issue of slack budgeting by focusing on how information distortion takes place in the context of decision making. More specifically, the intent is to explore the extent to which accountability as a situational variable and self-monitoring as an individual characteristic provide a context conducive to slack budgeting (i.e., information distortion in a budgeting context).

6.2 SLACK BUDGETING AND INFORMATION DISTORTION

The literature on organizational slack shows that managers have incentives to create slack in their environment.[7,8,9,10,11,12] The literature on budgetary slack considers the budget to be the embodiment of that organizational environment and, therefore, assumes that managers will use the budgeting process to bargain for budgetary slack. As stated in the accounting literature, "managers will create slack in budgets through a process of *understating revenues and overstating costs*." Various studies report on the phenomenon of slack budgeting in organizational contexts.[13,14,15,16,17] Each of these studies seem to suggest that budgetary slack involves a deliberate distortion of input information. Distortion of input information in a budgetary setting arises, in particular, from the need of managers to accommodate their expectations about the kinds of payoffs associated with different possible outcomes. The link between the distortion of input information and the subjects' accommodation of their expectations is provided by agency theory and risk aversion. Given the existence of differential incentives and informational asymmetry between the controller (or employer) and the controllee (or employee), and the high cost of observing employee skill or effort, a budget-based employment contract (i.e., employee compensation is contingent on meeting a performance standard) can be pareto superior to fixed pay or linear sharing rules (where the employer and employee split the output).[18] However, budget-based contractual schemes create risk for the employee because his or her job performance may be affected by a host of uncontrollable factors. As a result, risk-averse individuals may resort to slack budgeting through systematic distortion of input information. In addition, any enhanced (increased) risk aversion would, in practice, lead the employee to resort to slack budgeting. The amount of slack is related to both the uncertainty and the expected value of future outcomes.

6.3 IMPACT OF ACCOUNTABILITY

The enhancement of risk aversion and the resulting distortion of input information may be more pronounced when accountability is high. Accountability is the degree to which an individual is responsible for a particular outcome. People who are accountable and expected to justify their decisions are inclined to perform the difficult, cognitive tasks considered to be signs of good decision making. Examples include the consideration of variety of options and impressions,[19,20] consistency in judgment,[21,22] and investment of more time and effort.[23]

In addition, accountability is linked to the management of information and impressions.[24] With high accountability, there is greater use of defensive information and more emphasis on positive aspects of decisions.

Could it also be concluded that slack budgeting through information distortion may be a defensive behavior arising from enhancement of risk aversion caused by a high accountability situation? A person in a high-accountability situation would be more risk averse than others and would be ready to resort to any behavior to cover the situation. As a result, he or she might attempt to distort the input information in order to have an attainable budget. This is in line with evidence showing that information distortion is a commonly observed tactic in studies of managerial respondents. Accordingly, the first hypothesis can be stated as follows:

H1: Individuals placed in conditions of high accountability will introduce more slack into estimates than individuals placed in low accountability.

6.4 IMPACT OF SELF-MONITORING

Similar to the accountability case, the enhancement of risk aversion and the resulting distortion of input information may be more pronounced when self-monitoring is high. Self-monitoring refers to the degree to which individuals attempt to control the images and impressions that others form of them during social interaction. High-self-monitoring individuals, out of concern for the situational and interpersonal appropriateness of their social behavior, are particularly sensitive to the expression and self-presentation of relevant others in social situations and use these cues as guidelines for monitoring their own verbal and nonverbal presentation.[25,26] Moreover, "they are sufficiently skilled actors that they can successfully translate their beliefs about what constitutes a situationally appropriate self-presentation into a set of verbal and non-verbal expressive actions that convincingly portrays the right person for the situation."

Research on information distortion has revealed that high self-monitors are more likely to manipulate information to hide failures and to select positive information that gives others a better impression.

Could it be also concluded that slack budgeting through information distortion may be a defensive behavior arising from enhancement of risk aversion caused by a high-self-monitoring situation? A high-self-monitoring individual would be more risk averse than others and would be ready to resort to any behavior to cover the situation. As a result, he or she may attempt to distort the input information in order to have an attainable budget. Accordingly, the second hypothesis can be stated as follows:

H2: High self-monitors will introduce more slack into estimates than low self-monitors.

6.5 INTERACTION BETWEEN ACCOUNTABILITY AND SELF-MONITORING

The preceding discussion indicates that the situational characteristic of accountability and the individual characteristic of self-monitoring may encourage slack budgeting. As a result, the following interaction hypothesis is offered:

H3: There will be an interaction between accountability and self-monitoring such that high-self-monitoring persons in conditions of high accountability will introduce more slack into estimates.

6.6 METHOD

6.6.1 Subjects

The subjects where seventy-six male and female executives enrolled in a graduate accounting education course at the University of Minnesota. These executives agreed to participate in the experiment. They were told that they were participating in a study in "estimating aptitudes," and were guaranteed full confidence and anonymity. The average age of the participants was 32.96 years. The highest and lowest ages were, respectively, 56 years and 23 years. The average number of years of experience was 5.039. The highest and the lowest number of years of experience were, respectively, 25 and 2 years.

The participants were randomly assigned to either a high- or low-accountability condition and were given information about the experimental task. Each participant was assigned the role of the controller of a manufacturing company. The scenario was a budgeting problem. Participants were given the central role in making the budgeting decision. A final series of questions containing the self-monitoring instrument and background questions followed.

6.6.2 Experimental Task

The experimental task is similar to the one used by Cyert et al.[27] The experimental material included one page for instructions, one page defining the role of the participant, two pages for a paper-and-pencil task requiring the subjects to make cost and sales estimates, one page for the self-monitoring instrument, and one page for background information.

The instructions stated

> The purpose of this experiment is to evaluate the determinants of "estimating aptitudes." In order to get a true measure of a person's estimating ability, it is necessary to keep in mind the estimation's objective function, which is just to ensure that the budget is *attainable* and, second that the budget is *accurate*. In order to accomplish this, I am having you engage in the estimation of both costs and sales for a fictional company introducing a new product. It is important that you keep the estimation's objective function in mind when making your decision.

The second page was used to define the accountability conditions. Participants in the high-accountability condition were given the following instructions: "The controller is out of the country this week. You have been asked to act as a temporary controller. *You are responsible* for any decisions you make today. Your performance will be considered in your job evaluation and future career promotions. How will you handle the estimation problems in the next two pages?"

Participants in the low-accountability condition were told: "The controller is out of the country this week. You have been asked to act as a temporary controller. *You are not responsible* for any decisions you make today, nor will your job performance evaluation or future career promotions will be affected. How will you handle the estimation problems in the next two pages?"

The last two pages of the experimental material included a paper-and-pencil budgeting test requiring each subject to make ten estimates on the basis of the estimates of others. Two versions of the budgeting tests were presented: a cost version and sales version. The cost version reads as follows:

> Assume that you are replacing the controller of a manufacturing concern considering the production of a new product. You are required to submit your estimate of the unit cost of the product if 500,000 units are produced. Your two assistants A and B, in whom you have equal confidence, presented you with preliminary estimates. For each of the cases below, indicate your estimate of costs you would submit.

The sales version reads as follows:

> Assume that you are replacing the controller of a manufacturing concern considering the production of a new product. You are required to submit your estimate of the sales volume of the product if the price is set at $10.80. Your two assistants A and B, in whom you have equal confidence, presented you with preliminary estimates. For each of the cases below, indicate what estimates of sales you would submit.

Each question was followed by a list of ten pairs of numbers, representing the ten pairs of estimates by the two subordinates. The experiment involved the choice between two estimates of costs and two estimates of sales. The cost estimates are indicated in Exhibit 6.1.

The sales estimates were similar in value except that the cost estimates were expressed in dollars and those for sales in units. However, the sales estimates

Exhibit 6.1
Cost Estimates Presented to Participants

Cases	A's estimate	B's estimate	Your estimate
(1)	$1.54	$6.75	$ _____
(2)	$8.42	$4.56	$ _____
(3)	$3.25	$7.52	$ _____
(4)	$1.25	$4.35	$ _____
(5)	$6.24	$4.70	$ _____
(6)	$1.80	$7.30	$ _____
(7)	$6.89	$1.65	$ _____
(8)	$3.25	$7.52	$ _____
(9)	$4.74	$1.54	$ _____
(10)	$3.20	$5.35	$ _____

were presented in various different orders to obscure the similarities in values. One such order of sales estimates is indicated in Exhibit 6.2. Upper and lower limits of ten pairs for costs ranged from multiples of 125 to multiples of 842 and included two pairs in which the difference was approximately a multiple of 200, two pairs in which the difference was approximately a multiple of 300, two pairs in which the difference was approximately a multiple of 400, two pairs in which the differences was approximately a multiple of 500, one pair in which the difference was a multiple of 521, and one pair in which the difference was a multiple of 386.

6.6.3 Self-Monitoring Scale

Participants completed the self-monitoring scale, a set of twenty-five true-false self-descriptive statements that measure individual responsiveness to social cues. The set included items that describe (1) concern with the social appropriateness of one's self-presentation, (2) attention to social comparison information as cues to appropriate self-presentation, (3) the ability to control and modify one's self-presentation and expressive behavior, (4) the use of this ability in particular situations, and (5) the extent to which the respondent's expressive behavior and self-presentation is cross-situationally consistent or variable. The instrument has been found to have a multifaceted dimensional scale that predicts social behavior. Scores ranged from 1 to 20. The mean and standard deviation for the self-monitoring scale were 11.56 and 4.38, respectively. The coefficient alpha reliability estimate for this scale was 0.56. A median split pro-

Exhibit 6.2
Sales Estimates Presented to Participants

Cases	A's estimate	B's estimate	Your estimate
(1)	320,000 units	535,000 units	$ _____
(2)	474,000	154,000	$ _____
(3)	325,000	752,000	$ _____
(4)	689,000	165,000	$ _____
(5)	180,000	730,000	$ _____
(6)	624,000	470,000	$ _____
(7)	125,000	435,000	$ _____
(8)	325,000	752,000	$ _____
(9)	842,000	456,000	$ _____
(10)	154,000	675,000	$ _____

cedure (median = 13.10) was used to transform self-monitoring into a dichotomous variable (low, high) for purposes of data analysis.

6.6.4 Post-Experimental Questionnaire

All participants completed a questionnaire testing the efficacy of the experimental manipulation as well as providing background information. The manipulation check question inquired whether the participant perceived himself or herself as accountable for the experimental decision. The background information included age, gender, and number of years of managerial experience.

6.6.5 Design and Analyses

The two levels of accountability conditions (low, high), the two levels of self-monitoring (low, high) and the two types of budgeting decisions (cost and sales estimate) resulted in a $2 \times 2 \times 2 \times N$ factorial design. The seventy-six subjects were randomly assigned to the accountability conditions and exposed to the two different scenarios: the sales and cost scenarios. Subjects were designated as low or high on the individual characteristic of self-monitoring based on whether their score fell below or above the median value. The nature of the task is assumed to lead the subjects to build slack. First, it asks for an attainable budget. Second, the courses being taken by the subjects emphasize the notion of biased payoff schedule within an organization. Therefore, if the payoffs are perceived to be biased or if they are perceived to depend on considerations other than the relations between the estimate and the true value, the tactical decision on biasing the estimate becomes more important to the estimator.

6.7 RESULTS

6.7.1 Manipulation Check

Results showed that participants in the high-accountability condition ($M =$ 17.50) reported that they felt greater accountability than those in the low-accountability condition ($M = 9.20$), $F(1, 148) = 180.52$, $p < 0.001$, $w = 0.67$.

Each subject's cost and sales estimates E were transformed into a summary statistic x, which represented the weight assigned to the larger of the two given numbers in the pair presented to the subject such that

$$E = xU + (1-x)L$$

where U is the upper number and L the lower number.

The use of a linear combination of the two estimates was considered superior to a single reliance on the mean. In effect, the summary statistic x highlights the bias brought by the subject to his or her estimates better than the use of the

Exhibit 6.3
Summary Analysis of Variance

Source of Variation	df	SS	MS	F value
Model	7	4.70508	0.67215	18.15*
A. Budgeting Decision	1	0.52934		14.30*
B. Accountability	1	0.16577		4.48**
C. Self-Monitoring	1	0.18414		4.97**
A.B.C.	4	3.82582		25.83*
Error	144	5.33322	0.37029	
Corrected Total	151	10.0372		

° Significant at $\alpha = 0.01$
°° Significant at $\alpha = 0.05$

mean estimate. It is used in this study as the data for the analysis of variance. The mean estimate does not highlight the bias because it gives equal weight to the observations.

6.7.2 Effect of Accountability and Self-Monitoring

The analysis of variance is summarized in Exhibit 6.3. The main effects were significant. The nature of the level of accountability, the type of budgeting decision, and the level of self-monitoring each had a significant impact on the weight assigned to the largest estimate at $\alpha = 0.05$. The interaction effect was also significant at $\alpha = 0.0001$. The nature of the interaction effect is indicated by an inspection of the cell means which are shown in Exhibit 6.4. A response of 0.5 is unbiased and responses greater than 0.5 for cost estimates and less than 0.5 for sales estimates represent slack creation. Exhibit 6.4 indicates that slack appears to be created in (1) cases of high accountability, (2) cases of high self-monitoring, and (3) cases of high accountability and self-monitoring. The patterns of the results support the three hypotheses.

6.8 DISCUSSION

These results suggest that (1) subjects in either high accountability of high self-monitoring and (2) high self-monitoring in conditions of high accountability resort to slack budgeting through information distortion in the budgeting process.

Exhibit 6.4
Means of Cells Summary Table

a. Panel A: Accountability and Self-Monitoring

	Low Accountability		High Accountability	
	Low Self-Monitoring	High Self-Monitoring	Low Self-Monitoring	High Self-Monitoring
Costs	0.25928	0.42526	0.52631	0.79500
Sales	0.67785	0.41263	0.36083	0.30684

b. Panel B: Accountability

	Low Accountability	High Accountability
Costs	0.35484	0.67627
Sales	0.52515	0.33697

c. Panel C: Self-Monitoring

	Low Self-Monitoring	High Self-Monitoring
Costs	0.41303	0.63162
Sales	0.46424	0.38372

These results support earlier empirical findings that sales and costs tend to be estimated with a bias, even though the bias might be in a different direction for each type of estimate and that estimates within a complex decision-making system involve attempts by estimators to control their payoffs. The difference arises in the nature of the motivation for slack behavior. Our results show that the bias introduced by the estimators is more prevalent in cases of high accountability and high self-monitoring. One possible interpretation is that slack budgeting behavior occurs as a result of an enhanced risk aversion due to high self-monitors being placed in situations of high accountability. Both high accountability and high self-monitoring appear to accentuate risk aversion, leading to distortion of input information.

6.9 CONCLUSION

Certain hypotheses on slack budgeting were derived from an examination of the impact of accountability and self-monitoring on the distortion of input information. First, high accountability and high self-monitoring have an impact on organizational estimation decisions. Second, high self-monitors placed in situations of high accountability will resort to a slack budgeting behavior.

NOTES

1. G. R. Ferris and K. M. Kacmar, "Organizational Politics and Affective Reactions," Paper presented at the 30th Annual Meeting, Southwest Division of the Academy of Management, San Antonio, Tex., 1988.

2. R. Allen, D. Madison, L. Porter, P. Renwick, and B. Mayes, "Effective Organizational Communication," *California Management Review* 22 (1973): 77–83.

3. D. Caldwell and C. O'Reilly, "Responses to Failure: The Effects of Choice and Responsibility on Impression Management," *Academy of Management Journal* 25 (1982): 121–136.

4. C. O'Reilly, "The Intentional Distortion of Information in Organizational Communication: A Laboratory and Field Investigation," *Human Relations* 31 (1978): 173–193.

5. Mark S. Young, "Participative Budgeting: The Effect of Risk Aversion and Asymmetric Information on Budgetary Slack," *Journal of Accounting Research* (Autumn 1985): 825–842.

6. William S. Waller, "Slack in Participative Budgeting: The Joint Effect of a Truth Inducing Pay Scheme and Risk Preferences," *Accounting, Organizations and Society* (December 1987): 82–98.

7. L. J. Bourgeois, "On the Measurement of Organizational Slack," *Academy of Management Review* 6, no. 1 (1981): 29–39.

8. Richard M. Cyert, J. G. March, and W. H. Starbuck, "Two Experiments in Bias and Conflict in Organizational Estimation," *Management Science* (April 1961): 254–264.

9. Harvey Leibenstein, "Allocative Efficiency vs. 'X-Efficiency'," *American Economic Review* (June 1966): 392–415.

10. A. Y. Lewin and C. Wolf, "The Theory of Organizational Slack: A Critical Review," *Proceeding: Twentieth International Meeting of TIMS* (1976): 648–654.

11. L. R. Pondy, "Organizational Conflict: Concepts and Models," *Administrative Science Quarterly* 12, no. 2 (1967): 296–320.

12. J. V. Singh, "Performance Slack and Risk Taking in Organizational Decision Making," *Academy of Management Journal* (September 1986): 562–585.

13. M. Dalton, *Men Who Manage* (New York: John Wiley and Sons, 1961).

14. R. M. Barefield, "A Model of Forecast Biasing Behavior," *The Accounting Review* (July 1970): 490–501.

15. A. E. Lowe and R. W. Shaw, "An Analysis of Managerial Biasing: Evidence from a Company's Budgeting Process," *Journal of Management Studies* (October 1968): 304–315.

16. Mohamed Onsi, "Factor Analysis of Behavioral Variables Affecting Budgetary Slack," *The Accounting Review* (July 1973): 535–548.

17. Kenneth A. Merchant, "The Design of the Corporate Budgeting System: Influence on Managerial Behavior and Performance," *The Accounting Review* (October 1981): 813–825.

18. J. S. Demski and G. A. Feltham, "Economic Incentives in Budgeting Control Systems," *The Accounting Review* (April 1987): 336–359.

19. S. Chaiken, "Heuristic Versus Systematic Information Processing and the Use of Source Versus Message Cues in Persuasion," *Journal of Personality and Social Psychology* 39 (1980): 752–766.

20. P. Tetlock, "Accountability and the Complexity of Thought," *Journal of Personality and Social Psychology* 30 (1983): 526–537.

21. G. Cvetkovich, "Cognitive Accommodation Language and Social Responsibility," *Social Psychology* 41 (1978): 149–155.

22. R. Hagafors and B. Brehma, "Does Having to Justify One's Decisions Change the Nature of the Judgment Process?" *Organizational Behavior and Human Performance* 31 (1983): 223–232.

23. P. McAllister, R. Beach, and T. Mitchell, "The Contingency Model for the Selection of Decision Strategies," *Organizational Behavior and Human Performance* 24 (1979): 228–244.

24. Patricia M. Fandt and Gerald R. Ferris, "The Management of Information and Impressions: When Employees Behave Opportunistically," *Organizational Behavior and Human Decision Processes* (February 1990): 140–158.

25. M. Snyder, "Self-Monitoring Processes," in L. Berkowitz, ed., *Advances in Experimental Social Psychology*, Vol. 12 (New York: Academic Press, 1979).

26. M. Snyder, "The Self-Monitoring of Expressive Behavior," *Journal of Personality and Social Psychology* 30 (1974): 526–537.

27. Cyert, March, and Starbuck, "The Experiments in Bias and Organizational Behavior."

SELECTED BIBLIOGRAPHY

Allen, R., D. Madison, L. Porter, P. Renwick, and B. Mayes. "Effective Organizational Communication." *California Management Review* 22 (1979): 77–83.

Barefield, R. M. "A Model of Forecast Biasing Behavior." *The Accounting Review* (July 1970): 490–501.

Bourgeois, L. J. "On the Measurement of Organizational Slack." *Academy of Management Review* 6, no. 1 (1981): 29–39.

Caldwell, D., and C. O'Reilly. "Responses to Failure: The Effects of Choice and Responsibility on Impression Management." *Academy of Management Journal* 25 (1982): 121–136.

Chaiken, S. "Heuristic Versus Systematic Information Processing and The Use of Source Versus Message Cues in Persuasion." *Journal of Personality and Social Psychology* 39 (1980): 752–766.

Cvetkovich, G. "Cognitive Accommodation, Language and Social Responsibility." *Social Psychology* 41 (1978): 149–155.

Cyert, Richard M., J. G. March, and W. H. Starbuck. "Two Experiments in Bias and Conflict in Organizational Estimation." *Management Science* (April 1961): 254–264.

Dalton, M. *Men Who Manage*. New York: John Wiley and Sons, 1961.

Demski, J. S., and G. A. Feltham. "Economic Incentives in Budgeting Control Systems." *Accounting Review* (April 1987): 336–359.

Fandt, Patricia M., and Gerald R. Ferris. "The Management of Information and Impressions: When Employees Behave Opportunistically." *Organizational Behavior and Human Decision Processes* (February 1990): 140–158.

Ferris, G. R., and K. M. Kacmar. "Organizational Politics and Affective Reactions." Paper presented at the 30th Annual Meeting, Southwest Division of the Academy of Management, San Antonio, Tex., 1988.

Hagafors, R., and B. Brehma. "Does Having to Justify One's Decisions Change the Nature of the Judgment Process?" *Organizational Behavior and Human Performance* 31 (1983): 223–232.

Leibenstein, Harvey. "Allocative Efficiency vs. 'X-Efficiency.' " *American Economic Review* (June 1966): 392–415.

Lewin, A. Y., and C. Wolf. "The Theory of Organizational Slack: A Critical Review." *Proceeding: Twentieth International Meeting of TIMS* (1976): 648–654.

Lowe, A. E., and R. W. Shaw. "An Analysis of Managerial Biasing: Evidence from a Company's Budgeting Process." *Journal of Management Studies* (October 1968): 304–315.

Lukka, Kari. "Budgetary Biasing in Organizations: Theoretical Framework and Empirical Evidence." *Accounting, Organizations and Society* (February 1988): 281–302.

McAllister, P., R. Beach, and T. Mitchell. "The Contingency Model for the Selection of Decision Strategies." *Organizational Behavior and Human Performance* 24 (1979): 228–244.

Merchant, Kenneth A. "The Design of the Corporate Budgeting System: Influence on Managerial Behavior and Performance." *The Accounting Review* (October 1981): 813–825.

Merchant, Kenneth A., and Jean-Francois Manzoni. "The Achievability of Budget Targets in Profit Centers: A Field Study." *The Accounting Review* (July 1989): 539–558.

O'Reilly, C. "The Intentional Distortion of Information in Organizational Communication: A Laboratory and Field Investigation." *Human Relations* 31 (1978): 173–193.

Onsi, Mohamed. "Factor Analysis of Behavioral Variables Affecting Budgetary Slack." *The Accounting Review* (July 1973): 535–548.

Pondy, L. R. "Organizational Conflict: Concepts and Models." *Administrative Science Quarterly* 12, no. 2 (1967): 296–320.

Schiff, M., and A. Y. Levin. "The Impact of People on Budgets." *The Accounting Review* (April 1970): 259–268.

Singh, J. V. "Performance, Slack and Risk Taking in Organizational Decision Making." *Academy of Management Journal* (September 1986): 562–585.

Snyder, M. "Self-Monitoring Processes." In L. Berkowitz, ed., *Advances in Experimental Social Psychology* 30 (1974): 526–537.

———. "The Self-Monitoring of Expressive Behavior." *Journal of Personality and Social Psychology* 30 (1974): 526–537.

Tetlock, P. "Accounting and the Complexity of Thought." *Journal of Personality and Social Psychology* 30 (1983): 526–537.

Waller, William S. "Slack in Participative Budgeting: The Joint Effect of A Truth Inducing Pay Scheme and Risk References." *Accounting, Organizations and Society* (December 1987): 82–98.

Young, Mark S. "Participative Budgeting: The Effects of Risk Aversion and Asymmetric Information on Budgetary Slack." *Journal of Accounting Research* (Autumn 1985): 825–842.

Index

About the Author

AHMED RIAHI-BELKAOUI is Professor of Accounting at the College of Business Administration, University of Illinois at Chicago. A member of the editorial boards of several professional journals, he is author or coauthor of more than 25 previous Quorum books.

DATE DUE